The Last Ten Pounds

❧

With Love & Gratitude,

Lina Sage

September 30, 2016

The Last Ten Pounds

ONE WOMAN'S JOURNEY TO LOVE (BY
SHEDDING FEAR, ANGER, HATRED...
AND EVERYTHING IN-BETWEEN)

⚘

A Memoir
Lina Sage

ISBN: 1533347654
ISBN 13: 9781533347657
Library of Congress Control Number: 2016908653
CreateSpace Independent Publishing Platform
North Charleston, South Carolina

For Dad. May you rest in peace.

"The wise need not do anything but to surrender to the eternal void that is nothingness."

- LINA SAGE -

Fear

PROLOGUE

❧

"Uncle Quinn... please stop. Please stop, Uncle Quinn! Stop it, you're hurting me!" I wailed loudly.

"Shhh... I'm just playing with you," he replied with a sly look on his face, as he continued to grope me with both hands.

This had happened many times before, the constant touching and fondling of my private parts every time Uncle Quinn saw me. See, the thing is, I didn't make it easy for him because of my feisty nature. Usually I would be able to run away before he could really get ahold of me and on the times that I couldn't get away, his inappropriateness would only last a few minutes until I would squirm so hard that he would finally release me from his grasp.

But today was different and I felt it immediately. His huge hand pinned down both my tiny wrists and with his other hand he proceeded to maliciously rip off my summer jumpsuit. His weight crushed my petite frame to the floor so much so that I couldn't move. No matter how hard I tried, I couldn't create enough wiggle space to escape his 6'2" lanky stature. With his free hand he pushed his fingers inside me with such ferocity that a loud scream escaped my mouth before I could even discern what was happening.

This was so different from the other times. All the other times he was gentler. It was just rubbing and touching but today it was so painful I couldn't bear it.

"Uncle Quinn... stop it! Stop!" I continued to beg as I lay there sobbing uncontrollably.

He didn't stop nor did he respond to my cries; instead, he kept forcing his fingers up there, repeating his actions, each time leaving a greater indentation. The pain was so excruciating that my cries grew progressively louder but even that didn't manage to get any reaction from him.

When he did finally stop, it gave me brief hope that the terror was over, but it was only to unzip his pants to pull out his package.

Oh God, oh God... oh God, make him stop! What is he doing to me?

I don't remember ever feeling this scared before in my entire life. The fear I felt in this moment was so paralyzing that it made the fear I felt when Dad would come home drunk and bash Mom's head against the wall seem inconsequential.

In a rhythmic manner he continued to finger rape me while masturbating to it. It seemed like my colossal fear, combined with my crying pleas, was the catalyst that turned him on even more – like it wasn't only the sexual violation but the power he had over me and his awareness that I couldn't do anything to defend myself. When he finally unloaded his bodily fluids on me, he pulled himself off and flashed me a bright smile as if nothing had happened. He didn't say a single word as he pulled up his zipper and made his way downstairs.

My small mangled body lay there for a few minutes until I finally garnered the strength to pull myself up. Immediately my legs felt weak and wobbly and the burning sensation of my raw and chafe vagina made me fall down again. I was soaked in his sperm and sweat but managed to hold myself up long enough to wipe myself clean from all traces of him.

What did I do? Why did he do this to me?

I limped slowly downstairs to find Mom in the kitchen cooking.

"Mom, Uncle Quinn touched me down there and it really hurts. Can you tell him to never do that again? I don't like him," I sobbed loudly.

"What do you mean he hurt you? He's just playing with you!" Mom yelled.

"Well, I don't like the way he plays with me!" I shrieked back.

"How dare you speak to me in that tone and how dare you disrespect your uncle," Mom replied, raising her hands and whipping me with the chopsticks she was cooking with.

"Why do you have to scream and cry all the time? I can't have one single minute of peace in this house?" Mom screeched as she continued to beat me with the chopsticks. I guess she was having a bad day because she unleashed all her rage on me, repeatedly whipping me with those chopsticks with such force that she didn't stop until one snapped in half and fell to the floor.

"Mom, stop! I'm sorry," I cried while holding both my arms up against my face to protect it.

"Go to your room and I don't want to hear about your uncle anymore!" she instructed.

I carried my beaten body back up the stairs to my room and out of the corner of my eye I saw Uncle Quinn sitting on the sofa with an invincible look on his face. I curled my body into a fetal position and cried myself to sleep all the way until the next morning. When I awoke, the six-year-old girl that I was the day before no longer existed. Whoever that little six-year-old girl was meant to grow up to be just simply vanished. I believe there's a moment in everyone's life when a situation occurs that can change the course of your destiny. Usually it happens later in your adult life or at least when you're old enough to comprehend things, but with me it happened that fateful day. That moment changed my life forever.

Even at such a young age, in that moment, I felt like something inside of me had died. Because my brain was too young to understand actions, all I had to go by was how I felt. And how I felt was a deep sense of violation, like someone had robbed me of something so sacred. I also felt immensely rejected by my mother and felt that she had made it pretty clear that she loved Uncle Quinn more than me. All I desperately wanted was for Mom to believe me for once and to comfort me. I wanted Mom to kick Uncle Quinn out of our house instead of always telling me that he's living with us to help pay bills. Mostly, I just wanted to feel safe in my own home rather than the gut-wrenching anxiety and fear I felt on a daily basis.

The abuse continued on for many years. It included a lot of fondling and rubbing of my genitals. His attempts at making me perform oral sex on him as I got older failed miserably because I made sure to keep my mouth wired shut to avoid him forcing himself in. Not to undermine his abuse, I was lucky in some ways because he never penetrated me with his penis. I don't know if I would have survived if that had happened.

When I was feeling strong enough, I would fight him off me and he would let me get away. Other days when I wasn't as strong, I would surrender to the unjust and lie there until he had finished satisfying himself. Afterwards my best and only coping mechanism was to sleep it off. Every time he abused me I felt like he would take a little part of me away. Eventually all those little parts added up to where I felt nothing. I never told Mom of the continued abuse because in my mind if she didn't believe me the first time, then she wasn't going to believe me now.

So I continued on with my life just as my parents had taught me. I went to school and said nothing to my friends or teachers. One day I showed up to school with a perfect palm imprint on the side of my face that Uncle Quinn had so graciously given me.

My parents told me, "If the teacher asks what happened, tell them you fell." I eventually became an expert liar whenever there was a bruise on me I couldn't hide. They say it's good for children to have routine. My routine was going to school every day trying to excel academically to avoid getting beaten by my mom for being stupid; meanwhile trying to hide the fact that my dad was an abusive alcoholic and that my uncle repeatedly molested me.

CHAPTER 1

☙

"LINA! CAN YOU HEAR US? Lina, wake up! How old is the patient?!" I heard someone frantically ask.

"She's fifteen!" another voice replied.

I tried to open my eyes but my eyelids felt so heavy and blinded by the bright fluorescent lights that I was unable to keep them open for long.

Am I in heaven?

"Lina... you're in the hospital. Can you tell us what you took tonight?" a man in green scrubs asked me.

"Pills..." I replied groggily.

"Yes... we know, but what kind of pills? How much did you take?"

"I... I... don't know."

"Okay, we're going to give you some charcoal and it's going to make you throw up. You'll feel nauseous from it but everything will be okay."

I lay there in and out of consciousness, throwing up a foul-tasting concoction until my stomach burned in its own acidity. I didn't care so much as to the fact that I was hooked onto a whole bunch of foreign machines that were beeping away and that all the people buzzing around me were trying to keep me alive. The fact that my sister Carmen was right by my side, stroking my hair as I continually threw up or the fact that Mom was standing beside us sobbing didn't even register. Whatever lucid thoughts I was able to conceive were all about if Miguel was there. Then just like that, I fell into an abysmal sleep.

I don't know how long I slept, but when I awoke I was greeted by a friendly woman. "Hi Lina," she said. "You're okay. You're in the hospital because last night you took a whole bunch of pills. Your mom and sister are here. I'm going to go get the doctor."

Still feeling disoriented, I tried to sit up, but my throbbing headache and the weakness of my body made me fall back, pinching the IV in my arm.

"Lie down. You're weak," Carmen said. She then tried to make me comfortable as she made way for the doctor entering the room.

"You're a lucky girl," the doctor said, examining me with his stethoscope. "You took enough Tylenol 3 to kill yourself, but luckily you got to the hospital just in time. Your liver is damaged so you'll have to stay in the hospital for a week so we can monitor things and get you some psychiatric help."

"Psychiatric help? What does that mean? I feel okay, doctor. Can I go home now?" I asked in a weak voice, still not fully grasping my actions from the previous night.

"I'm sorry, but you tried to take your own life last night. That's serious stuff. We want you to talk to a psychiatrist so that she can help you deal with any issues you have in your life that would lead you into thinking that suicide is the only way out."

There's nothing wrong with me. I'm just heartbroken. Is Miguel here? Does he even know I'm in the hospital?

"Listen to the doctor. He's right," Carmen chimed in.

As soon as the doctor left, I turned to Carmen and asked, "Where's Miguel?"

"He's not here. I talked to him this morning to tell him that you were in the hospital but he said he was too busy to come and see you. Listen, the guy is an asshole. He's not worth your time. He obviously doesn't care about you but we do. What you did last night scared the shit out of us... and over a guy?" Carmen spoke gently.

Just like that, my already shattered heart broke again for the millionth time. Miguel was my first love and my only love up until now. It was destiny that brought us together. How else can you explain the fact that we only lived a house away from each other? He was my savior of sorts because he offered me a sense of security that no man in my life had ever been able to do. In the six months that we had been together, all the incessant bullying that I had been experiencing at school seemingly vanished due to the fact that I was Miguel's girl.

He was the only guy that had ever given me the time of day. And our endless phone conversations only solidified the fact that he truly cared about me.

Miguel was a sixteen-year-old 'bad boy' whose suave and charismatic personality made him the popular guy. Everyone liked him. In addition, he was the only one at the time with his own car. Not to mention, he provided access to buy alcohol and cigarettes to all his friends with his fake ID. All this added to his uber-cool persona. He was very attractive with his dark skin, full lips, and great sense of fashion which only made him that much more desirable to all the girls. So the fact that he would pay attention to me and want to be with a not-so-cool girl like myself made me feel like the most special girl in the world.

Our worlds instantly merged the moment we were introduced at the mall. We spent an entire summer being completely inseparable. If a love spell existed, I was definitely under it. It only took a couple of weeks before I had fallen madly in love with him and him with me. I remember the first time he told me he loved me. We were a couple of hours into a heated make-out session. He stopped and whispered into my ears, "I love you." Those three words completely melted my heart. I finally felt a sense of validation, like I was worthy enough for someone to love me. I couldn't remember ever feeling happier.

Naturally, when Miguel and I were in the back seat of his car and he asked me to make love to him, the thought petrified me. But, the notion of losing Miguel because I wouldn't have sex with him was so frightful that it dictated my inability to say no. I agreed and gave up my virginity to Miguel even though I knew we were moving too fast. My mind justified it by convincing myself that what we have is true love and that we were going to be together forever. After we graduate from high school we would get married and, unlike my parents, we would have the perfect marriage. He would protect me from all harm, but most importantly he would love me unconditionally.

So when Miguel abruptly broke up with me a couple of weeks earlier by telling me that he didn't love me anymore, my whole existence was utterly destroyed. The one person that I felt loved and protected by did not want anything to do with me any longer. I trusted him enough with my delicate soul to lose my virginity to him. Wasn't that supposed to bind us together for life? Was I too naïve to believe that?

The pain became so unbearable that all I wanted to do was die. I didn't see the sense of living anymore. I felt like every guy I ever trusted in my life has hurt or abandoned me. I was an empty vessel just walking about trying to make sense of what I had done wrong for Miguel to stop loving me. It was a desperate attempt for Miguel to see that he had made a big mistake and that we did in fact belong together but at the same time, without even realizing it, it was a desperate plea for help from what was happening at home.

"What would we do if you died?!" Mom wailed. "How would I live without you? You're fifteen years old. There will be plenty of other guys in your life. Why would you do something so stupid?" Mom cried while Carmen quietly stood there holding my hand.

But I only want Miguel.

Mom's open affection surprised me as I had never seen this side of her. As Mom and Carmen said their goodbyes, promising they would come back tomorrow to visit, I let my tired self fall back into another deep sleep.

CHAPTER 2

✂

WITH MY BODY STILL FEELING fragile, the nurse pushed me in a wheelchair down to the psychiatrist's office. I was physically and emotionally exhausted and I was in no mood to talk to anyone about my issues. Seeing a therapist was only for wacky people and even though I did try to kill myself, I still declared myself sane.

If only I could talk to Miguel... explain things to him. If he comes back to me, then all this pain will go away and I'll be happy again.

I was greeted by an older woman whose face showed me enough compassion as she asked, "How are you feeling today?"

"I'm fine," I lied.

"Okay," she hesitated. "Well, can you tell me why you're here?"

I sat there quiet for a long time before the psychiatrist broke the silence and said, "Listen, you don't have to be scared. Everything we talk about will be confidential. Nothing will leave this room. I'm here to help you."

"It's nothing really..." I stammered. "My boyfriend and I broke up and I was so sad. I... I... just wanted to get his attention. I didn't really want to die."

"Okay. Can you tell me more? Are there things happening at home that make you unhappy?"

There was a long, awkward silence again before I lied and said, "No, every-thing is fine."

The look on her face clearly showed me that she didn't believe me. So, she switched gears and asked me, "Tell me something interesting about yourself. Were you born here in Canada?"

"No, I was born in Vietnam but came to Canada when I was one. My family… we were boat refugees."

"Boat refugees?" she asked.

"Yes, we escaped Vietnam by boat. That's how we came here," I said.

"That's interesting. Can you tell me more?" she urged.

The story of how we came to Canada is a story that Mom and Dad liked to tell my siblings. They would continually remind us that they didn't risk their lives so that we could come to Canada to become underachievers.

It was a remarkable story of sorts and reiterated just how fortunate we were to have made the journey. In 1979, even though the Vietnam War had ended four years prior, the country was still suffering socially and economically. Shortly after I was born, Dad decided that the conditions in Vietnam were damaged to the point beyond repair. He wanted to escape the country. Dad especially hated the communist ways and in order to provide a new and better life for us, the only thing he could do was try to put together an escape plan to leave Vietnam for good.

During those times, people tried to escape Vietnam on a daily basis. Some would try to go by foot and cross the border into Thailand and others would try to escape by boat. The lucky ones ended up making it to a refugee camp where they would stay until they were accepted to another country. Those who didn't make it would risk their lives and die in the journey. A lot of the boats were caught by the Viet Cong and sent back to Vietnam where the people would be sent to jail to rot. Some boats simply vanished, while others would run out of food and one-by-one, everyone on the boat would die. Others were robbed by pirates where they would beat the men senseless and rape the women. Chances of survival were slim to none, and only those who were lucky enough made it.

It took him months to put together a plan that involved escaping by boat. It was a dangerous mission, but Dad thought the risk was worth it. To him, living in Vietnam at the time was like a death sentence. Dad teamed up with the help of a local villager who had a fishing boat. The plan was that the man would supply the boat while Dad would supply the fuel and food. Our family didn't have any money to buy such supplies, so Dad started selling seats on the boat to others in the village for a small fee. With that money, he slowly started buying fuel. He had to hide the fuel underground so that the Viet Cong wouldn't catch on to what they were doing. Each time fuel was bought they would find a spot and bury it. He also got people to start rationing out their food. He told them to put away rice and potatoes as well as collecting and hiding well water.

Everything was working out and the plan was to leave right after "Tet" – the Vietnamese New Year. Tet typically occurs in January or early February. The truth was, nobody knew how to keep track of the weather patterns, but typically every year the winds would be calm after the Tet holidays. So, the plan was to leave immediately after. Unfortunately, that year, the winds continued on well after Tet, so we didn't leave until much later.

On the evening of March 10, 1980, in the middle of the night, my family along with others escaped Vietnam. In total there were sixty people (men, women and young children) on a tiny fishing boat. We were crammed in like sardines and there was still not enough room. Nobody wanted to be left behind, so out of desperation and panic, people started throwing water and fuel overboard to make room for their families.

We were out at sea for three whole days before we reached the international line. During those three days we were blessed with perfect clear skies and not a breeze of wind. Unfortunately, because most of the drinking water had been thrown overboard, everyone was suffering from severe dehydration and by the fourth day, the situation on our boat was dire. We were now completely out of water. People were starting to drink the salt water. Even though there was still food on board, without water there was nothing to cook with. In addition, the cramped conditions on the boat, underneath the sweltering hot sun, only amplified the discomfort. Just when everyone thought they were doomed, a miracle happened.

Off in the distance, Dad spotted an oil drilling rig. Luckily for us, one of the men on our boat worked as a translator during the war and spoke decent English. They refused to let us onboard because they were not a rescue boat. However, they were kind enough to load us up on supplies and direct us in the proper direction towards Malaysia. We loaded up our tiny boat with all the fresh fruits, water, and fuel they gave us. Then, we were on our own again. For the first time in two days all the babies onboard, including myself, had stopped crying while their mothers continued to nurse them with their renewed hydration.

Another full day passed before we came across a large vessel. As we pulled in close, we realized that this was the supply boat that made its weekly rounds to the surrounding oil rigs. Dad knew that it was our only hope. It was now or never. He did something really gutsy and broke our boat's engine with full knowledge that international law states all capable boats must rescue ship-wrecked boats. His plan worked because they took all sixty of us onboard their ship. They fed us, provided showers for us, and dropped us off at a refugee camp where we stayed for seven months until Canada accepted us.

"Wow! What an amazing story," marveled the therapist.

"Are we done for the day? I'm feeling very tired," I complained, not wanting to talk anymore.

"Yes, we're done if that's all you want to share for today. We'll pick back up in a couple of days once you feel more rested," she replied sympathetically.

CHAPTER 3

⚘

A COUPLE OF DAYS LATER, I was back in the psychiatrist's office with the same lady.

"How are you feeling today?" she asked with concern.

"Better," I replied.

The last two days were occupied with me being in and out of sleep, only waking up when the nurses and doctor came in to check up on me. In those times, I would see my family there. Mom and Carmen were a constant fixture. The occasional times I saw Dad and my two brothers. But there was still no Miguel.

Maybe he'll come tomorrow.

"That's good. I'm glad you're feeling better. Lina, can you tell me a little bit about your childhood?" she asked.

What does she want to know?

The vulnerable state I was in made me want to reach out to the kind stranger. But it was engrained in me to avoid the truth when asked about what was happening at home. I was raised with the fear that if the authorities ever knew about my parents' domestic violence, then I would be taken away to live with strangers. Even though my home life was not ideal, the notion of living with strangers was enough to scare me from betraying my family.

My reluctance to talk only fueled her probing as she continued, "Are you scared to talk to me? Do you think something bad will happen if you talk to me?"

"No," I replied, looking down on the floor to stop myself from crying.

"It's okay," she continued. "Just take your time. We don't have to talk if you don't want to. We can just sit here all session but you might feel better by expressing your feelings. You've just gone through a traumatic breakup. I understand."

When I heard the word 'breakup,' the flood gates opened and the tears came pouring down.

"It's okay," the psychiatrist said as she wrapped me in her arms to console me. "You loved him a lot, didn't you?"

"Yes, but he still left me," I lamented as my heart continued to feel the pain as if it was fresh.

"Why do you think you love him so much?"

"Miguel's my first love and I thought we had something special. He said we were going to be together forever and I trusted him. I trusted that he would never leave me and then he just up and abandoned me. The worst part is, I don't even know why," I bawled.

"Is this the first time that someone has made you feel abandoned?"

I sat there with my face buried into my hands not wanting to think or feel anything. But being with her and in that office brought an upsurge of childhood memories that were filed deeply in the back of my subconscious. As a young child, it didn't take long for me to realize that Dad's only source of comfort was alcohol. His addiction caused him to leave me at home by myself on plenty of occasions. But before he left the house, I would always attach myself to his ankle and howl at him not to leave. The guilt of leaving his three-year-old daughter at home by herself must have gotten to him because he would lie and say he was going to the store to buy me ice cream. Each minute that I sat and waited for Dad to come home felt like an eternity. And, every car that drove by was false hope. The anxiety that I felt waiting endlessly for my father petrified me. I felt so alone because what is a three-year-old supposed to do by herself? By the time Dad made it home it would always be with empty hands as he was too drunk to remember the ice cream. It was always broken promises with him and somehow my first experience with a boy had been one of broken promises as well.

"Yes," I lied.

"Why else do you love Miguel?" she asked.

"Because he made me feel safe. He was like my security blanket, and with him I felt like I belonged somewhere," I replied.

"Do you feel safe at home?" she continued.

Do I feel safe at home? If she only knew.

My mind wandered back to the night when I was five years old and Dad came home in his usual drunken rage. He proceeded to go into the kitchen to grab a knife to butcher Mom into a million pieces.

"I'm going to kill you, bitch!" Dad screamed at Mom repeatedly.

Never one to back down with her mouth, Mom tempted, "I'm right here. What are you waiting for? You're nothing but a worthless drunken asshole!"

"No, Dad... put down the knife... please... put down the knife...," my siblings and I begged. We stood with our knees shaking, trying our very best to protect Mom, knowing that his violent outbursts were only directed towards her and never at us.

Dad managed to shove and lock us kids in the bedroom, but not before he locked Mom out of the house in the bitter cold of winter, wearing only a night-gown. Needless to say, the police were called to our house again, but this time instead of giving Dad a warning, they decided to arrest him and take us some-where safe. I should have felt protected now that we were away from Dad, but despite what he continually put us through, and our lack of security, I still loved him. I didn't want anyone to hurt him just as I didn't want him to hurt Mom. As bad of a drunk as he was, he was the polar opposite when he was sober. He was a kind and loving husband... a perfectly great father who taught me how to ride a bike and tie my own shoelaces.

It was that constant push and pull of good husband versus bad husband that would pull on Mom's heartstrings and make her stay. That and the fear of rais-ing four young kids as a single mom in a foreign country whose language she barely spoke was what kept her with him.

At times I often wondered if having no dad was better than having a dad that put his family through so many panic-stricken nights. And in return, it spawned a deeply resentful wife whose only outlet to release her own anger was on her children.

"Lina! Did you hear me? Do you feel safe at home?" the therapist asked, interrupting my thoughts.

"Um... yeah... everything is fine. I feel safe," I deluded again.

"Were you and Miguel intimate?" the therapist continued to probe.

"Umm... yes," I replied as I bowed my head down.

"It's okay," she replied tenderly as if sensing the embarrassment I felt in my admission to her. "Is this the first person you've been intimate with?"

Does Uncle Quinn count?

Uncle Quinn's escapades had stopped a few years earlier when he decided that my puberty-ridden body did not turn him on anymore. The abuse was something that I was determined to forget now that it was over. As long as I could make my mind believe that it never happened, well then it never happened. I learned from my parents that denial is the best coping mechanism.

"Yes," I replied again avoiding eye contact.

"How's school going for you? Do you have a lot of friends?" the therapist continued.

"School's okay. I've got a good group of friends now but before Miguel and I started dating the kids were really mean to me."

"How so?"

"You know... making fun of me because I'm Asian. They would pick on me whenever they wanted to. Well, not just me... basically every ethnic kid in school would get bullied," I replied.

"How would they bully you?" the therapist asked earnestly.

"You know... they would make fun of what we eat... what we wear. They would call us names like 'chink' or 'paki'."

"And how did that make you feel?"

"Of course I hated it, but what was I supposed to do? If you try and stick up for yourself then they pick on you even more, so you're better off ignoring them but some days are so hard," I responded, tearing up.

"Is that why being with Miguel made you feel safe?" the therapist asked in a soft voice.

"Well, yes. He was popular and most of the kids were scared of him. When we started dating... like overnight... everyone was so nice to me and it made me feel so good. Now he's gone…" I said, trailing off. "I don't want to talk anymore. Is it okay if I go back to my room?"

"Sure. We can pick up in a few days. Get some rest now," the therapist urged.

CHAPTER 4

⚭

THE REST OF MY STAY in the hospital was uneventful. My family were my only visitors. Every day I prayed that it would be the day that Miguel would come and see me so that I could rid myself from the deep void I felt without him in my life. Not having Miguel in my life dug deep into my biggest fear of being alone. And I hadn't yet connected it to the abandonment I felt from Dad as a child. At fifteen years old my consciousness could only grapple with the direct problem at hand. I needed a solution to the problem as opposed to relating it to 'why I ended up like this.'

My strapping fear of being alone only amplified my other fear of being so inadequate that no one would love me. By Mom choosing Uncle Quinn over me and now with Miguel gone, I was certainly convinced that I had no qualities that could make anyone love me. I was someone who was not worthy of love. How else could I explain Mom's and Miguel's rejection? But still I yearned for Mom's approval and for her to be proud of me. Getting out of the hospital meant that I had to work harder academically to make something out of my life.

As for Miguel, by the time I walked into the therapist's office for my last visit, all hopes of us getting back together had completely vanished. The illusion of the stability I perceived from being with him was only to satisfy the craving I desired for a stable upbringing. I realized that if killing myself was not a big enough reason for him to show any concern, then he truly didn't love me. I swore to myself that I would never let a guy break my heart again. In that, I convinced myself that love was somewhat of a fantasy and it didn't really exist.

"So how are you doing?" the psychiatrist asked.

"I'm feeling much better. I'm glad to be going home," I responded.

"Okay, so is there anything you want to talk about today?"

"No, not really. I just want to go home. I'm fine," I lied.

"Listen, Lina. I'm here to help you but I sense that you're afraid to tell me more. I can't force anything out of you but I feel like there's a lot more going on than just Miguel. I want you to take my card and know that I am here if you want to continue our sessions. I'm hesitant to give your doctor the clear to release you, so promise me…"

"I promise I'll call you if I need to talk. Trust me – I just did a really selfish thing over a stupid guy. I've learned my lesson. I swear," I interrupted in my most persuasive voice.

"Okay…," she replied hesitantly. "Well then, you're good to go."

The truth was I was still in denial that I needed any kind of therapy and I just wanted to forget about Miguel and anything bad that had happened to me. So after my release from the hospital, I stayed in that opulence of denial for a long time before unforeseen events made me climb out of my comfort zone.

Anger

❧

(Hatred, Resentment, Denial, and Everything In-Between)

CHAPTER 5

∽

FLASHING RED LIGHTS AND TURBULENT commotion outside made me abruptly wake up to a scene of a dozen men who were heavily armed, dressed in black armor and gas masks, jumping out of what looked like black SWAT vans. I was anesthetized in my own trepidation; unable to run or hide. All I could do was stand by my window. As if in slow motion—taken straight from the movies—I watched these men approach my house. You couldn't engage in an illegal grow op for long without getting busted and I had enough marijuana plants in my house to face a strong conviction. In that moment, my usually rapidly thinking brain experienced the unusual phenomenon of an out-of-body experience where time stood completely still and I felt like I was listlessly floating amongst the clouds. Harps played in the background replacing the loud bangs of the SWAT team trying to break down the door. And just as if I was protected by a sea of angels, I slowly came back to my body and realized that the loud bangs were that of my neighbor's door and not mine. The SWAT team had veered off to my neighbor's house without me even realizing.

As I let out a long exhale, I sprinted down to the basement, passed rows and rows of perfectly groomed marijuana plants, until I reached the breakers and proceeded to flip them off. The entire operation had to be shut down, regardless of how damaging it would be on the plants, just in case the men carried geo-thermal guns and could detect excessive heat coming from my house.

Back upstairs, I positioned myself by my window to keep a watchful eye. My heart was still racing as I peered through the windows but the men were nowhere to be seen. The two vans that came in were still parked—with their lights flashing amber. I assumed they were inside my neighbor's house now, which got me to thinking about what illegal activities they were up to. I'd only been living in my house for six months, and the truth was, I only bought it to start my grow op. The entire time I lived there, I'd only seen my neighbors the few times they pulled their minivan into their garage. I didn't even know who lived there or what they looked like.

Slowly, when my heart slowed down, and my nerves un-tingled, I couldn't help but wonder how I managed to pull this all together and how a twenty-three-year-old could run a full-fledged marijuana grow operation.

It all started eight months prior, when I was still living with my best friend Tanya. One day out of the blue, Tanya came home distressed. It looked like she was on the verge of crying, so I sat her down and asked her what was going on.

She sighed and then blurted out, "I've been growing pot with Dean for the past three months. We were so close to harvesting our first crop. But, then he left the basement window open last night. This morning, all the plants had died! We were supposed to make $20,000 off that harvest and now it's all gone. I'm so mad at him!"

I couldn't believe what I was hearing. I would have never suspected in a hundred years that Tanya was growing pot. We'd been best friends since high school and Tanya was always more book smart than she was street smart. She trusted people way too easily and was always against any kind of drug activities. So the fact that Tanya was growing pot was shocking. But Tanya's bizarre actions as of late made perfect sense now — from her absence at home to random things missing around the house to her asking me for a few months' rent in advance.

Dean was a tall, obese fellow in his fifties that Tanya had worked with in her previous job at an ad agency. Even though there was a significant age gap between them, they became fast friends. Tanya was attracted to how worldly and intelligent he was. Even though I didn't like him and thought he was just trying to get in Tanya's pants, she reassured me that they were nothing but friends and that he had a girlfriend back in the Philippines. Dean's much younger girlfriend in the Philippines had milked him out of his life savings and now he was completely broke. He came to Tanya asking for her help but Tanya was broke as well.

Like me, they were both tired of living paycheck to paycheck and wanted a quick way to make money. They got together and threw around some ideas. The one that stuck was to start up a grow op. Tanya had some childhood friends that she had kept in touch with that were involved in the business and could get them set up. When you grow up in a low-income area as Tanya and I both did, you always knew someone who was involved in the drug business.

Dean was all over the idea like moths to a flame. Almost immediately, he went out and rented a house to start on their new business plan. Tanya's hook-up came over and set up the equipment for her and taught her and Dean how to grow pot. In return, he charged them a small fee. They both agreed that Dean would live in the house and take care of the plants. Tanya would go out and try to find buyers through her childhood connections.

It all sounded very good until they got to the operations side and started trying to grow these plants. They were supposed to have a crop in about two months' time but Dean continually messed up on things that would stunt the plants' growth and delay the harvesting of the buds.

Apparently these marijuana plants were very finicky—it was imperative that these plants run on a consistent feeding and sleeping cycle. The "babies," as Tanya called them, liked to be fed based on a specific feeding chart and slept on a twelve-hour awake and twelve-hour sleep schedule. On their awake cycle, all the lights must be fully turned on, and on their sleep cycle, all the lights are to be turned off so the room would be pitch-black.

Dean, proving that he had the intelligence of a five-year-old who couldn't figure out math, was feeding the babies the wrong amount. Initially, they weren't growing as quickly as they should. Then on various occasions he would completely forget to set up the timer so their sleep cycles weren't uniform. On the night before they were supposed to harvest and get their big payday, Dean, being the overweight guy that he was, found the house overwhelmingly hot and decided to keep the windows open for some fresh air. He ended up falling asleep until the next morning and by the time he woke up to check on the babies they were completely wilted and dead. It had been -30°C out the night before and the babies didn't stand a chance.

What also got Tanya so irate was the fact that when the plants have full buds and are ready to harvest, they amass a very strong smell. Take the smell of the weed you occasionally smoke and times that by hundreds of plants—you can imagine how overpowering the smell could be. The fact that Dean kept the windows open potentially could have exposed the smell to the neighbors who could have called the cops on them. But that was besides the fact that a buyer was lined up to purchase the inventory.

Why on earth would she go into business with Dean?

"The guy is so stupid," Tanya cried. "I should have never done this with him. He always seemed so smart. I didn't think anyone could possibly be this dumb! What should I do now? I maxed out all my credit cards to get this thing up and running. I needed that money to pay bills."

I sat there quietly, not knowing what Tanya could do. Her crop was gone and there was nothing she could do to save it. All I could think about was how much money she could have made and that got me thinking that I wanted in on a potentially lucrative business. My mind whipped into a frenzied vortex and all of a sudden my thoughts wouldn't shut off.

I'm already looking for a house to buy. I can turn the basement into a grow op. Tanya can show me how to grow and we can do it together. All she has to do is take the set up and put it in my basement and we can be partners. Dean just needs to fuck off.

"How much did you say you can make off this?" I asked.

"Well, if you have good quality pot, it'll sell for around $1800/pound but it can go as low as $1500/pound for the shitty stuff."

"How often can you get a crop?"

"About eight weeks but I hear it can be as soon as six weeks."

"How much would it cost to set up everything?"

"Well, it depends on how many lamps you want and how big you want the operation. Why are you asking me all this?"

"Because I want in. I'm sick and tired of living paycheck to paycheck. I've been looking for something to do that could make me some quick cash. This is perfect. I'll do it with you. We can be partners."

"Whoa! Wait a second! Are you sure?" Tanya asked. "Are you absolutely fuckin' sure? Because it's not as easy as it sounds and a lot of things can go wrong. What happens if we get busted?"

"Well, you didn't seem overly concerned about getting busted when you did it with Dean," I replied.

"Well, that's because the house lease was under his name. If anything happened, he would take the rap. Plus, I really don't care a whole lot about him but I don't want anything to happen to you or me."

"Well, what's the worst-case scenario if we were to get busted? Knock on wood of course. Is it jail time?"

"No, for first-time offenders it's just a fine and probation. They confiscate all your plants and equipment and that's about it."

"Well, it doesn't seem all that bad and it's a risk I'm willing to take if it means I'm going to get rich quick! So what do you say?"

"Well, okay," Tanya continued on hesitantly. "I think this might be able to work."

"We can grow it at the new house I'm planning to buy."

"We'll need as much space as possible in the basement," she said. "How big do you want to go?"

"Well, as big as we can. Let's fill up the entire basement. If we're going to risk it, then we might as well do it all the way."

"Um, okay. Are you sure?" Tanya asked again hesitantly. "You don't think we should start off smaller and eventually go bigger?"

"No, what's the point?" I responded. "If we have the space we might as well do the entire basement. Listen, since this is going to be in my house, if anything happens, I'll take the rap for it. I'll never mention you. I'll do what Dean had been doing and take care of these plants. You can go find the buyers and sell it. You still have buyers, right?"

"Of course I do," Tanya responded, this time with more ease.

"Well then, it's settled. That's what we'll do. We'll split all the costs and profits fifty-fifty."

"Sounds good," Tanya nodded. But I could tell by the look on her face that she still wasn't certain.

In no time I'll make my millions and buy everything and anything I ever wanted.

My overwhelming desire to get rich quick was to relinquish me of all the anger that I had pent up inside of me. I rationalized that money would be the only thing to make me happy. My ambition and desperation had overtaken any common sense and left me completely blinded by any danger I was getting myself into.

The rustling of footsteps snapped me back to my current reality. I was witnessing some of the men carrying black garbage bags with marijuana plants pouring out of the top. I couldn't believe what I was seeing. Had I known that my neighbor was growing pot, I would have never bought this house. But what I saw as an ideal location, being situated in a quiet family-friendly neighborhood with an affordable price tag, also seemed ideal for my neighbor. What are the chances of two houses on the same block growing marijuana? And why was I the lucky one that didn't get my front door kicked in?

CHAPTER 6

WITH THE WARMTH OF THE sun beating down through my windows, I sat up and threw my arms up in the air. I needed to stretch out all the kinks. I peered out my window hoping that last night was just a terrible dream but the loud yellow "DO NOT ENTER" tape that surrounded my neighbor's house confirmed that last night really did happen. I wanted to kick myself for having fallen asleep when my intention was to stay up and keep an eye on the raid.

"You better get your ass over here," I demanded as soon as Tanya picked up her phone.

"Why? What happened?" Tanya asked.

The thing about engaging in illegal activities is that it can turn a normally reasonable person into an ultra-paranoid mess. Before growing pot, I was the kind of person who was always oblivious to my surroundings. Now I was the kind of person who was constantly checking my rear view mirror when driving to make sure no one was following me. It didn't help that I also lived all alone. My boyfriend, Beaver, was always out of town working and only came to visit every second weekend.

"My neighbor's house got raided last night by the cops. It was a marijuana grow op!" I shouted.

"You've got to be kidding!" Tanya exclaimed.

"Do I sound like I'm fuckin' kidding? Bring today's newspaper over too. I have a feeling this is going to be in the news."

As I waited for Tanya to come over, I found myself wandering outside to see if there was any other info I could find out. Sure enough, my neighbors were huddled together and talking amongst themselves.

"I can't believe someone would be crazy enough to grow pot here… there's a cop that lives right across the street," one neighbor asserted.

"What?! A cop lives right across the street?" I asked in surprise.

"Yeah, right over there," the man pointed. "And this manages to happen right underneath our nose."

Well, isn't it just my bloody luck?!

I walked back into my house shaking my head in disbelief. How in the world did I manage to buy a house next to an existing grow op? And on top of that, have a cop live across the street from me without even knowing?

This whole growing pot ordeal had been plagued from the first day. The plants gave us problems immediately: a bug infestation got us off to a slow start and affected our yield. What was supposed to be a ten-pound harvest turned out to be only five pounds of bad-quality pot, so we were only able to sell it for $5,000 which meant my big payday was only $2,500.

In our second harvest, we managed to produce a good ten pounds of high-quality THC pot. Tanya and I spent an afternoon trying our crop to test the quality. We weren't big stoners, so within minutes, we were high as a kite and giggling away like two school girls!

We were positive our new crop would be able to sell for the premium rate but the buyer took advantage of the fact that Tanya and I were two young rookies.

"The buyer says he'll give us $1,000/pound," Tanya said.

"What?! That's bullshit and you know it! We have good stuff this time!" I yelled.

"I know. I can't fuckin' believe it! He says it's because there's too much inventory."

"Too much inventory my ass! He's just trying to rip us off because we're girls!" I said.

"Yeah, I know. But what do you want to do? We need the money."

"I don't know. You know it's worth at least $1,800/pound. Do you know any other buyers?" I asked.

"No, I don't. I think we should just sell it and then I'll try to get us some new buyers for the next crop. We're both broke and you know we're desperate right now," Tanya replied.

Tanya was right but I still couldn't help but feel enraged. I knew that we were being cheated. This only fueled my disdain towards the world and how unfair everything was. It seemed the harder I worked, the more debt I was drowning in. All of my credit cards were maxed out. I was already behind on my mortgage payments. And that didn't include the mountains of bills that needed to be paid.

But the massive debt that weighed heavily on me was the money that I had borrowed from Mom to purchase the house. Mom had happily lent me the money for a down payment. I had promised to pay back the substantial loan within a year. Little did she know that I had used a part of the loan to get the grow op up and running and the hefty payday that I thought would come so easily has failed to arrive.

A couple hours later, Tanya arrived at my house with the newspaper.

"Listen to this," she started. "Apparently a neighbor had reported the house because the owners were coming in and out at odd times and it seemed like nobody was living there. They seized hundreds of marijuana plants that have a street value of over $500,000."

"What a load of shit!" I replied while Tanya nodded. It was just like the cops and media to inflate the prices of these actual drugs to make it seem like a massive drug bust. In actuality, it's never really that much. "I just can't believe how lucky you are!" Tanya uttered over and over again.

I was grateful that the world decided to throw me a bone for once, but that was not enough for me to call it even. As I saw it, the world had decided to screw me over a long time ago. In my mind, I was trying to absolve myself from my misery by doing something that was supposed to make me fast cash. Instead, the world decided to throw obstacles in my way to refrain me from getting to my happiness. Why wasn't I allowed to sleep in a bed full of cash and be blissful for once? Why was the world so dead set on having me be the bitter person that I was?

CHAPTER 7

꼭

TANYA AND I DECIDED TO play it safe and keep the lights off for another couple of days until the cops had finished their business next door. The interruption ended up stunting the growth of the plants and delayed the harvest by two weeks. By the time the buds looked ready for harvest, we decided to keep them under the lights for an additional week in hopes of bulking up the smallest bud size.

On the day of the harvest, Tanya and I sat down on our little stools and began the long and tedious process of trimming the leaves. An hour into trimming and the sauna-like heat combined with the circulating dust was making it inconceivable to breathe. Just when things couldn't get any worse, I noticed a web-like cloud on some of the buds. At a closer glance, there was no disputing that it was mold. We had made the wrong call to leave the plants under the lights for an additional week. I couldn't believe I didn't notice the mold in the past week while watering the plants but it wasn't obvious until you looked closely.

"Great! It's one thing after another with this shit!" I shouted.

"Well, let's keep going and see what we can salvage," Tanya said optimistically

"I'm so sick of this! This is not working out as I thought. I'm so done with this shit!"

"What do you mean you're done?"

"Look, we're still sitting on ten pounds from the last crop because our buyer has disappeared off the face of the earth. I mean it's bad enough that he has been ripping us off but now he's nowhere to be found. What's the point of growing this shit if we can't even sell it?! I just want to shut everything down."

"I know. I feel the same too, but how are we going to get out of debt?" Tanya asked.

"I don't know. Sorry, I'm just beyond stressed and I know you are too. I just don't even know what to do anymore."

"Well, let's just focus on what we have to do now and I'll continue trying to find a new buyer for our stuff. Everything will be okay," Tanya replied, trying to console me.

That was the great part about Tanya—she always knew how to be strong for the both of us. But for the most part, Tanya was notoriously always more optimistic than I was... choosing to see the glass as half full rather than half empty. It was with that attitude that made Tanya instantly likeable by everyone. I, on the other hand, walked around with a huge chip on my shoulder, wary that people couldn't be trusted. This explained why I loathed people and didn't have many friends while Tanya was the life of the party. In fact, Tanya's friends often wondered how she could be so close to someone like me, but Tanya saw beyond my tough exterior and knew full well that I was deeply misunderstood. The tough shield that I wore was only to protect myself from getting hurt.

I wanted desperately to believe that everything would be okay, but I wasn't convinced. I wanted out of this mess but I just didn't know how. After Tanya left that evening, I lay in bed reeking in my own self-loathing and blaming myself for being stupidly ambitious. I cried buckets until my eyes were sore and until my nose hurt from blowing it so hard. I was scared of getting busted and I wasn't sure how I was going to pay off my insurmountable debt. Thoughts of shutting down the operation flashed through my mind but that was a luxury I couldn't afford. I had to suck it up and continue on, hoping that it would all work out.

Just when I was about to fall into my depression sleep, the ringing of my phone woke me up.

"Hi babe. How are you?" Beaver asked enthusiastically.

Of course Beaver wasn't his real name. It was a nickname that Tanya had made up for him. We would refer to Beaver behind his back, which seemed like a mean thing to do, but we couldn't help it. Beaver had the misfortune of being born with the worst case of buck teeth you've ever seen. They were complete with a very wide gap separating his two front teeth. His smile was almost comical looking and resembled that of a beaver's. So within weeks of dating, that nickname kind of stuck.

Beaver and I met through my sister, Carmen, and had been together for a couple of years. I was instantly attracted to Beaver's upbeat personality and wry sense of humor. But because there was no physical attraction it took everyone by surprise when they found out that we were dating. The truth was I didn't really care whether or not I was attracted to him—I just didn't want to face my fear of being alone. After Miguel, I had gone from one relationship to the next to avoid the emptiness I often felt and Beaver proved to be a great distraction. It also didn't hurt that he loved me enough to stand by me when I told him about my plans to grow pot.

"I'm so stressed!" I wailed loudly.

"Is there anything I can do?" Beaver asked sympathetically.

"I need some money to pay the mortgage and bills and to live," I replied.

"I'll send you some money. I don't have much but I can send you $1,000 for now. Is that okay?"

"Thank you. That means a lot to me."

"Hey, don't worry. Everything will be fine. I'm here for you, babe. You know I love you, right?"

"I know," I replied.

CHAPTER 8

ॐ

TWO DAYS AFTER TRIMMING THE leaves, Tanya and I finished the harvest by spreading the buds out on the floor to dry. Then we began the other arduous task of cleaning up and replanting. This was before the time of hydroponics. We were still doing it the old-fashioned way... by soil. This entailed emptying copious amounts of soil into garbage bags and dragging it up the stairs into my trunk to dispose of at a landfill. The process had to be repeated many times because there was only so much my small sedan could carry. By the third trip my dainty arms and legs would succumb to the heavy duty lifting. Luckily for us, Tanya's athletic build and strength were so much more beneficial to the process.

We ended up getting eight pounds of weed, which was better than we anticipated, after we threw away the moldy buds. Now the next hurdle was to find a new buyer who would pay us a hefty price for our product.

Our prayers were answered when Tanya managed to get a new contact from an acquaintance. It turned out that the new contact was a middleman that would sell our product to the highest bidder, keeping a small percentage for himself. He insisted on us handing over our entire supply to him as opposed to the standard sample bag we would give out. Even though we knew this guy couldn't be trusted, when you're in dire need of cash, you go with the only option you have no matter how brash.

The twisted knots in my chest along with my constant headache and stomach pains pretty much left me incapacitated to think clearly let alone make any wise decisions. Even when I was feeling my worst physically, I kept persuading myself that it was all from the stress of the grow op. I was in complete denial of the fact that my bulimia had slowly crept back into my life like an old unwanted friend.

CHAPTER 9

೪

THE PREVIOUS YEAR TANYA HAD basically blackmailed me into therapy. It wasn't hard for Tanya to catch on to my bad habits especially when you live with someone and the walls are thin. When Tanya finally confronted me about my bulimia, I lied through my teeth convincing her that I'd only done it a few times and that I would stop even though I had no plans to stop. To me it wasn't that big of a deal and I saw it as a great way to control my weight in my quest to achieving perfection. The fact was, I wasn't anywhere near overweight, but it was always the quest to lose five pounds or to make X amount of dollars that gave me the perceived ideation of a wholesome joyous person.

Tanya gave me an ultimatum to either go to therapy or she would expose me to my family. I didn't want them to know because I didn't want Mom to view me as flawed. They had a hard enough time dealing with Carmen coming out as gay and confessing she was in a relationship with a woman. That had Mom crying as if someone had died and had Dad wanting to admit Carmen into a psych ward. If they were to find out about my bulimia, their hopes of having one normal daughter would vanish.

So I reluctantly agreed. A couple of weeks later, I found myself back in therapy for the second time in my life.

"Hi Lina. I'm Vicky. It's nice to meet you," the therapist greeted in a soft-spoken voice.

"Hi. It's nice to meet you," I replied as fake as ever.

"I've been counseling young women like yourself for ten years now. I know how hard it is to take that first step to get help. I'm very proud of you for that."

I so don't want to be here.

"So can you tell me a little bit about yourself?" Vicky asked.

There was a long pause from my end. "Well, what do you want to know?"

"Can you tell me a bit about your eating problem? My notes tell me that you binge and purge from time to time?"

"Yes," I admitted, "but I have it under control. I'm only here because my best friend Tanya thinks I need to get help but I think I'm doing okay."

"Well, how many times a day do you do it?"

"It used to be a lot more, like two to four times a day, but I've got it down to just once a day or every other day."

"That's good. You're making progress. How do you feel after you binge and purge?"

"Well, initially I feel good because I got rid of all the food that's going to get me fat but then afterwards I feel really sick... all the stomach acid and the nasty taste in my mouth."

"Then why do you do it?"

"Well, isn't it obvious? To control my weight!"

My God, is she dumb! Isn't that what every bulimic or anorexic person wants? To be skinny. We wouldn't be doing this to gain weight.

"I see," Vicky responded while writing down some notes on a paper pad. "How long have you been doing this for, or I should say, when did you start?"

"After high school. Around when I was twenty, so I guess two years now."

"What made you start?" she asked.

"Well, I wanted to lose weight because I was dating a guy who told me I was just average. I didn't want to be average. I wanted to be skinny like those models."

"Can you tell me how that made you feel when he said you were average?"

"Like shit! Who wants to be average? It made me feel like I wasn't good enough to be with him because I wasn't the perfectly skinny and pretty looking girlfriend. Just because I don't believe in love doesn't mean that I don't want to be loved and to feel important."

"Okay... very interesting," Vicky paused, "Have you lost significant weight over the past two years?"

"No. Not really," I replied disappointed.

"Did you know that bulimia is found in women of all shapes and sizes? It's those with anorexia who are ones that lose a significant amount of weight."

What the fuck? Is she encouraging me to be anorexic?

"The reason why I'm telling you this," Vicky continued, "is to let you know that in most cases bulimia isn't really about losing weight. It's more about control issues or emotional issues that could stem from childhood. Most of the time you couldn't even tell if someone was bulimic by looking at them because the women can be any size, but you can always tell if a person is anorexic. That's why bulimia most often is overlooked but it's just as damaging as anorexia."

That's true. I've never really thought of it that way.

"Do you feel like you always need to be in control of a situation?" Vicky continued on.

"Yes."

"Do you feel like this bulimia is a way for you to control certain aspects or things in your life?"

"Possibly."

"What do you think would happen if you gave up that control?"

"I don't know. I've never let it happen."

"What is it that you're trying to control?"

What is it that I'm trying to control? Well, what about my whole fucking life? If you can't even control what you put in your mouth, then you're a weak person!

"I don't know," I lied.

"What was your childhood like?"

"I don't want to talk about my childhood. I don't see how that's relevant to my problem," I responded, feeling agitated.

"Okay. Fair enough. Do you have a boyfriend, Lina?"

"Yes... his name is Beaver... we've been together for a while now," I replied, relieved that she changed the topic.

"That's great! How is your relationship with Beaver?"

"It's fine."

"Fine... okay... would you say you love him?"

What is she getting at?

"I don't believe in love."

"Why don't you believe in love?"

"To me love is like a drug. First it feels like euphoria but when it wears off, you crash and burn and are left feeling like shit."

"Okay. I've never heard that analogy before," Vicky paused and then continued. "But do you believe love exists?"

"Maybe for some people but not for me. I gave up on love a long time ago."

"Such a bold statement to make for someone so young. If you don't believe in love, then why are you with Beaver?"

"For convenience, so that I don't have to be alone. Plus, I know that he loves me and would do anything for me. It's safer to be loved than to love."

"I see," Vicky replied while jotting down more notes. "Tell me more about Beaver. What is he like?"

"He's just your average skinny white guy. He has a stable job working in IT. He's a little older than I am. He's twenty-nine but he looks young for his age, so I'm okay with it."

"What does his family think of your relationship? Do they accept it?"

"What family?" I retorted. "His dad basically left him to fend for himself after his mom passed away from a brain tumor. He was only thirteen at the time. He has an older sister but she moved out shortly after to live with her boyfriend."

"That's unfortunate. Why do you think Beaver is with you if you don't love him?"

"Just because I don't love him doesn't mean I don't care about him. Besides, he doesn't know that I don't love him. I mean, we tell each other that we love each other all the time; it's just that I don't really mean it on my end. Besides, as much as I say I'm with him for convenience, I think Beaver likes being with me because of my family. He keeps telling me that being with me makes him feel part of a family that he never had."

"And how does your family feel about him? Do your parents think the seven-year age gap is too much? Are they okay with the fact that you're dating outside your race?"

"They like him. After my sister Carmen came out as gay, my parents are just happy that I like guys."

"I see," Vicky continued scribbling down more notes. "How do you feel about your sister being gay?"

"It doesn't bother me one bit. I love my sister. She's always been there for me."

"So then you are capable of love. You love your family? Your sister?"

"Yes, but that's because it's my family. I'm incapable of loving another man!" I exclaimed.

"And why is that?" Vicky probed.

Oh God. I don't have all day to get into Miguel and Dad and Uncle Quinn.

"What does this have to do with my eating disorder? I thought I came here to get help on my bulimia, not talk about my love life," I responded.

"Are you generally a happy person?" Vicky asked changing the subject again.

"Not really. What's there to be happy about? I'm twenty-two years old, living with my best friend and just making ends meet."

"What would make you happy?"

"Having lots of money. People with money are always treated better."

"I see... have you been mistreated by people?"

"I just don't like people. I can't trust anyone. The world is a bad place and only the shrewd can survive," I responded curtly.

"You sound very angry. Why are you so angry at the world?"

Because I hate Uncle Quinn. I hate Dad. I hate Mom. I hate everyone!

"I don't know," I lied. "I guess it's just the way I am."

"Is this your first time in therapy?"

"Yes," I lied.

There's no way I'm telling her about my botched suicide attempt.

"Lina, I think it would be beneficial if you continued coming to see me on a weekly basis. We've covered some ground today but I feel like there's more we need to do for your recovery. Since you've acknowledged that you feel the need to control things in your life and the bulimia is one of them, I'm not going to stop you this week from throwing up what you've eaten. In fact, you have the control of how often you'd like to do it."

I shot Vicky a confused look. *What the fuck is she saying?*

"Yes, you can throw up as many times as you'd like this week but every time you have the urge to do it, you have to stop and think of who's really in control. Is it the bulimia or is it you?"

I nodded, still a little confused. This was not what I expected from therapy. I thought I would be fed all this nonsense about how to stop binging and purging and the kind of harm it inflicts on you. Not that I already didn't know because I had already suffered a torn esophagus and broken blood vessels in my eyes.

"Okay, our session is done for today. How about we meet again next week at the same time?"

"Sure," I replied, relieved that the session was over.

I never made it back to see Vicky again, convincing Tanya that the one session had helped me tremendously and I was now equipped with the tools I needed to help me recover. In truth, that session barely scratched the surface of my deeply troubled mentality. I should have continued therapy but I was so engulfed in a cloud of anger and hatred that it was impossible for me to accept any kindness or grace from life. My emotions were still trapped in my past even though life was moving along.

CHAPTER 10

৬৮

"AH! I'M GOING TO KILL that fucker!" Tanya bawled. "It's gone! It's all gone! He ran off with our pot and his number is disconnected."

It was two in the afternoon when I rushed over to Tanya's house only to find her strewn across her chaise lounge crying mercilessly into the sleeves of her pajamas.

"It's okay," I consoled, pulling Tanya's long black hair away from her face.

Heaven knows why I was so calm that day. But as Tanya continued to weep, I found the strength to be the strong one for the both of us. Everything that could have possibly gone wrong had gone wrong. Now we were left with nothing but a gargantuan amount of debt and the stress that came along with it.

"What are we going to do?" I asked rather calmly.

"I don't know. Do you want to shut it down? How much is your debt at now?" Tanya sniffled.

There's the money I owe Mom, the credit card debts, my default mortgage payments, overdue bills, and the money Beaver lent me.

"I'm over $50,000," I replied. "How about you?"

Tanya thought about it and then responded, "Around $40,000."

"I think we need to start thinking of a plan B," I urged. "I regret ever doing this. I know you tried to warn me but honestly I didn't think it would be this hard. I thought it was supposed to be easy cash."

"So you want to shut it down?" Tanya asked.

"Yeah. I'm done. I don't want to do this anymore," I responded. I was exhausted by the thought of having to endure the continual emotional rollercoaster.

"Well then, what are we waiting for? Let's tear it all down," Tanya replied. She looked like she had lost all sensibility. I've only seen this happen a couple times. But when I saw that look in her eyes, I knew better than to argue with her.

Tanya and I charged over to my house and proceeded to cut down every single pot plant. Basking in our temporary euphoria, and with heavy-duty scissors in our hands, Tanya and I didn't stop until every single plant was destroyed. When we had finished, it finally hit me the complexity of our grow op. For the first time in my life, I felt a sliver of gratitude towards whoever was watching over me the entire six months I was doing this. I should have felt more grateful towards this greater force; however, I was still living in the mindset of a victim.

When all was said and done, we managed to sell our equipment for a fraction of the cost. Within a week, my basement was completely empty with all traces of me ever growing pot vanishing. The only thing left to do was to figure out quickly what I was going to do to pay off my debt. Tanya and I ran ideas back and forth. She contemplated accepting an out-of-town job from a friend. All her accommodations and food would be covered which meant all the money she made could go directly to her debts. I, on the other hand, needed another means to make quick cash. I thought back to the easiest cash I ever made… giving a client named Gary a hand job for $1,000 during my days working as a mobile massage therapist.

CHAPTER 11

❧

GARY WAS A LAWYER WHO had been referred to me by a mutual client. Gary owned his own small firm and he covered everything from wills to real estate to family law. I was excited at the prospect of finally building some professional clients. Up until then, my clients were usually husband and wife, with the wife entrusting me, or shall I say her husband, to get massaged by me. Little did they know... their husbands would spend most of the time soliciting me, which only strongly supported my beliefs about men – that they couldn't be trusted. It didn't matter what age, race, or social background they came from; they all wanted the same thing – sex.

After doing mobile massage for a year, I noticed the same pattern with most of my male clients. It all had to do with the stereotypical fantasy of receiving a happy ending by a young pretty Asian masseuse. I would arrive at the client's house and present myself professionally, but in the back of my mind, I always knew what they were really thinking. What they wanted to say was, "My penis. Please just suck it, fuck it, or do anything for me to unload." But, they opted politely to tell me that it was their "glutes" that needed work.

I would continue with my usual talk of, "I'm going to leave the room so you can undress. Please lay face down in between the sheets with your face on the cradle."

I mean it was pretty much self-explanatory and anyone who's ever had a massage will know what I mean. The timid men would follow instructions but for the more brash, those instructions translated to them lying completely nude on top of the sheets with it all hanging out. This always led to me explaining to them that this was indeed a professional massage and there would be no happy ending. The really bold men did not hold back, always bluntly asking, "So, do you do any extras?" I almost preferred it that way because then I could be blunt with my answer and there would be no hidden agenda.

My excitement over Gary quickly evaporated when I stepped into Gary's office. Instantly, I was transported back to the seventies. His office was filled with mismatched and tattered furniture. If that wasn't hideous enough, when Gary opened up his mouth, he spoke almost entirely in slow motion.

"Hi Liiiiinnna…. it's sooooo nice to meeeeeeet you," Gary greeted. I tried not to laugh at his two-sizes-too-big plaid suit and thick-lensed glasses that were perched on top of his beak-like nose. I couldn't take him seriously as a respectable lawyer.

Gary was going through a divorce and loved to bitch about his toxic soon-to-be ex-wife. He complained how she was draining his bank account because he was supporting her expensive lifestyle including her stay in the Caribbean during the winter months – she hadn't worked a day in her life. His grown kids lacked ambition "just like their mother," he complained. So he had to support them as well.

"All this is so taxing!" he dragged on. "Oh Lina, that's why I need my massages from you to escape my life. It's sometimes just dreadful!"

I'll give it to Gary… he had a way of using words. If there was such a thing as a drama king, he would most definitely be crowned.

It didn't take long for Gary to come clean and confess his penchant for visiting Asian massage parlors. He divulged that in addition to seeing me twice a week he was also going to the massage parlors where the girls were more than eager to please him. I couldn't help but partially vomit in my mouth. I found him repulsive in every way. And, based on my previous experiences, I knew exactly where this conversation was headed.

"Oh Lina, I wouldn't have to visit those other massage places so often if you would add on to your services."

Gross! Just remain professional. You've dealt with this before.

A part of me wanted to laugh out loud and the other part of me wanted to kick him off the table and leave.

Of course you have to go to these parlors and get jerked off. You're so ugly, who the hell would want to sleep with you?!

"You know I only give professional massages, so you'll just have to keep going to those massage parlors."

"I know, but a man can only dream," he sighed.

I rolled my eyes so far back in my head I could have passed out from it.

What a loser!

On another occasion, after he ranted about his family, he continued to tell me how to save $200 a month on office supplies. According to him, this would equate to $2,400 a year. And over the course of ten years it would be....

This guy is completely off his rocker. Could he be any weirder?!

I shook my head as I continued to work the knot out of his back. Gary continued lecturing me about how law firms waste so much money on office supplies and how he had come up with a spreadsheet to be able to cut cost even down to a paper clip.

You're obviously not very busy if you spend your time making up spreadsheets to save money on a fuckin' paper clip. Man, is this guy for real?!

One day out of curiosity I asked Gary how much he would pay me for a hand job.

"Well, I pay $60 at the massage parlor," he replied. "But because you're so special Lina, I'll give you $100."

"Does that $100 include the massage as well or just for the hand job?" I asked.

"The massage parlor charges $60 for the massage and a happy ending," he slyly replied.

Wow – there are girls that are willing to give a massage and a hand job for $60?!

"Well Gary, there's no way you're going to get me to give you a massage and jerk you off at the end for $100."

"Well how much do you want?" he asked inquisitively.

"$1,000 bucks cash!" I blurted out. I knew that no one in their right mind would pay $1,000 bucks for a hand job and that would end the sexual harassment.

"A thousaaannnd dollars!" he exaggerated. "That's one expensive hand job. I think for that amount we should fuck!"

Ewe! Gross. Did he just say fuck? Hell no! I'd never in a million years sleep with this guy!

"No Gary, that's just for a hand job. If you can't afford my prices then maybe you should stop asking me for extras at the end of your massage and keep going to those other girls."

"Oh, but Lina I fantasize about you!"

Gross!!!

"Well, you can keep fantasizing."

I was certain that I had put an end to all his sexual soliciting. So during the following massage when Gary said, "Lina, I want you to give me a hand job! I'll pay you the thousand dollars," I felt like I'd been struck by lightning.

What the fuck! Did I just hear him say he'll pay me the $1,000 bucks for a hand job?

"You heard me. I'll pay you the $1,000," Gary demanded.

"Do you have it now? In cash?" I stammered nervously.

"Yes. It's in my safe." And with that he climbed out from under the sheet and exposed his nasty naked fifty-something-year-old body to me.

Oh my God, what have I got myself into!? Fuck he's so gross!

I wanted to pack up my things and leave. But, at the same time, a thousand bucks was a lot of money that couldn't have come at a better time.

You've given plenty of hand jobs before. Yes, but they were with boyfriends – not a paying client.

I struggled with my consciousness as I tried my best not to watch Gary's saggy ass saunter over to his safe. But, that didn't prepare me for the unsightly scene of his protruding belly and droopy balls as he turned around to walk back towards me.

Fuckin' gross, I can't do this! Yes, you can. It's $1,000 bucks and he probably won't last too long.

As he climbed up on the table, I went over to the light and dimmed it until it was almost completely dark. He was already hard by the time I got back and before I knew it I was stroking him back and forth for what seemed like far too long.

"Oohhh… that's right… a little faster…" Gary instructed. I tried to focus on all the things I could buy to keep from feeling totally disgusted with myself.

"Oh yes baby... oh yes baby... I'm gonna cum... I'm gonna cum," he moaned amidst a loud exaggerated screech—an over-the-top wail that sounded like he was going to pass out and die right then and there. Finally, a few drops of cum squirted out.

That's all?! Wow, all that moaning for a couple drops of cum?

"That was wooonnnddeerfullll. Thank yooouuu!" he said with a huge grin on his face.

I ran to the washroom, scrubbing my hands for a good five minutes. When I returned, a fully dressed Gary handed me the money. I scurried around packing up my things and wanted to leave as quickly as possible. I felt like the whole room was about to collapse on me and I needed some air to breathe.

Later on that evening, as I immersed myself in a hot bath, I couldn't help but have conflicting thoughts of how dirty I felt and how easy it was to make the money. Without insight, that event was a catapult into the sex industry for me because it unlocked what my mind had been conditioned to believe. If something as sacred as sex could be taken away so easily from me, leaving it of no value, then the only value that could be placed on it for me would come by the way of money.

CHAPTER 12

"I THINK I WANT TO get into escorting," I blurted out to Tanya.

"What?!" Tanya squealed. "I'm sitting here telling you that I'm going to take the out-of-town job and out of nowhere you tell me you're going to be an escort!"

"Remember that lawyer Gary I used to massage?"

"Yeah…"

"Well, he once paid me $1,000 bucks to give him a hand job and honestly it was the easiest thousand bucks I ever made."

"Seriously!?" Tanya replied. "Do you still see him?"

"No, that was only that one time and he hasn't called me since. Probably had buyer's remorse for spending so much money on a hand job," I laughed.

"You know what, there's no judgment from me. I hear escorts make pretty good money," Tanya said.

"How do you know?"

"Well, remember that old apartment I used to live in?"

I nodded and gave her that look to continue.

"The girl who lived across the hall from me was an escort."

"And she was open about it?" I asked in surprise.

"Yeah, she even handed me her business cards and asked me to pass them around. She told me she only worked a couple of nights a week and would make something like $10,000 a month!"

"Seriously!" I exclaimed.

"Yeah, and she wasn't even pretty or anything."

"What did she look like?"

"Well, she was blonde with big boobs. Kind of fat. Well, voluptuous I'd say. Not that tall either and probably in her thirties. Seriously, if she can make $10,000 a month off her looks you'll be more than fine."

"Yeah, but did she have to sleep with all the guys she goes out with?"

"Well, I'm assuming, but I don't know. I didn't really ask her about that."

"See, that's the thing. You always hear that escorts or strippers or phone sex operators make such good money but what if it's all bullshit? Look at us. We heard growing pot makes you good money and look at where we are now," I replied.

"Yeah, I know. Are you sure this is something you can handle? Because I'm sure all these girls end up sleeping with all their clients."

"You know me. I don't really care about the sex. And I don't put my emotions into it. It would just be a job to me and as long as it pays well enough, then I don't really care."

"Well, you know I'm not going to encourage you to do it but if that's what you decide to do, then all I can do is support you."

"Thanks, I appreciate it," I replied, so grateful that Tanya was in my life.

"But what do you want to be? Escort, stripper, or phone sex operator?"

"Well, definitely not a stripper. I can't dance worth shit and I don't want anyone I know to see me. Besides, just the thought of guys throwing loonies and toonies at you... that would hurt so bad."

"I know. I agree."

"I could do the phone sex operator thing, but I don't even know where to start with that. It's not the kind of job where you just walk in and apply. You know that friend of a friend you told me that does it? How did she get started?"

"I don't know. I just heard through a friend. Who knows if this is even true?"

"See it's always hearing things through the grapevine. Well, the easiest is the whole escort thing. I'm just going to Google some escorting agencies in the city and see if they're hiring. But honestly, I don't even know how much I'm going to make. Maybe I'll try the escort thing for a couple of months and see how it goes and work somewhere else at the same time."

"Are you sure you don't want to go and work with me?"

"No, that's your thing. You go do that. I'll try this out and see how it goes."

"What are you going to tell Beaver?"

"I'll tell him the truth," I replied honestly.

"What if he doesn't want you to do it?"

"Well then, we'll just have to break up."

Just as with my grow operation, I made the decision to get into escorting without much thought of how it was going to impact my life. The only emotion that came along with my decision was the cynicism of how much money I would actually make. I didn't want to fall into the same trap of believing that I could make quick cash only to find out the hard way again.

That afternoon after Tanya left, I Googled escort agencies. A few popped up and I decided to call the one that advertised that they had been around for the longest.

"Hello," I stammered. "I was wondering if you're hiring."

"We're always looking for new girls," a woman in a rough voice replied. "Have you done this before?"

"No," I replied nervously.

"Even better. Come down tomorrow morning at 10:00 and we can talk. My name is Pam," she instructed.

Was that a job interview? Why was it even better that I had no experience?

CHAPTER 13

❦

As I PULLED MY CAR in front of the building where Pam had given me the address, I was taken over by nausea. A glance in the rearview mirror reflected a fledgling girl who was struggling with herself.

What the hell are you doing? Giving a hand job is one thing but having to fuck for money is another. It's not too late to go home.

The frigid temperature and howling wind chill outside paralleled how I felt inside and I questioned how I even got here in the first place. Sure, it was the considerable debt that made me feel like I had been thrust into a desperate corner but unknowingly it was so much more than that. The desperation came with the energy of wanting to release all the excruciating pain and anguish that had been building inside me my entire life. Instead of stopping to take a real look at myself, I opted to believe that the world was going to somehow release my pain… that the world was the very reason why I was so shattered… and that the world would make amends and heal my wounds. Feeling empty inside impairs your ability to find any self-worth. So when it comes down to selling your body for money, it seemed hasty once the nerves settled.

You'll be fine. It's just a job. The oldest job in the world.

I walked up to the unassuming two-storey grey building that was located on a busy street. I had driven by this building plenty of times and had no idea what businesses it housed. There were no exterior signs nor were there numbers assigned to any of the offices. The only instructions I had was to walk up to the second floor and once at the top of the stairs to turn right and the office was the door to the right. I inhaled a deep breath and knocked gently on the door.

Here we go. Stay calm.

A few seconds later an unpleasant voice yelled, "Come in and make sure you take your shoes off."

I fumbled as I tried to take off my knee-high boots. I should have known better than to wear a dress when it was so cold out, but I wanted to make sure I looked my best. I even woke up early to curl my long hair.

"You must be Pam," I stammered as soon as I entered the office. "I'm Lina. We spoke on the phone yesterday."

Calm down. Don't be so nervous.

"Yeah. That's right. Have a seat," a plump women barked. "I'm the office manager here. I've been here for five years and basically take care of everything around here. The boss usually shows up once a week to pick up the cash. The way it works around here is we're open seven days a week from 7am-2am. When I'm not here, the girls sign up for shifts to man the phone. There's no pay for this but you get first dibs on general calls."

What's a general call?

"How much money can you make?" I asked straightaway.

"Well, it depends on how much you want to work. We don't make our girls work if they don't want to. It also depends on how marketable you are and I can say you're very marketable being all thin and pretty. Plus, you have the advantage of being Asian. You're gonna do very well. I have a knack for picking out the good ones," Pam chuckled, showing off her stained teeth.

"Do you get a lot of requests for Asian girls?"

"More than we can handle. There's only one Asian girl in the agency right now," Pam replied, pulling back her long, straggly grey hair.

"How many calls does she get during the week?"

"Ling does about five to six calls a day. The other ones who aren't so busy maybe do one call a day. Sometimes none."

"So you think I'll be busy?" I asked.

"I can guarantee you that you'll be busy. What days are you available?"

"Well, I can work every day but I was thinking of getting another job in case I didn't make much with this one."

"Forget the part-time job. You won't need it. All you'll want to do is sleep when you're not working. None of the girls here need a second job," Pam replied in an uncontrollable shrieking laughter.

"Can you tell me how much the girls make on average here?"

"Well, like I said, it depends on how willing they are to work and some girls make more because they have different specialties and are willing to do more. But Ling only works four days a week and she makes upwards of $20,000 a month."

Shit! Did she just say $20,000 a month?!

"Wow! Okay, sounds good. So when can I start?" I asked excitedly.

"You can start as soon as you go down to the city and get an escorting license. It costs about $100 and they'll also run a police check on you. That'll take a week and as soon as you're clear you can come back and see me. All our girls here have to be licensed and we don't employ anyone with drug problems. You have any issues I need to know about now?

"No."

"Well, good. In the meantime, you might want to think about names you want to go by. No one ever uses their real names."

"Names?"

"Yeah, names," Pam replied as if she was talking to a dummy, "The girls here usually create two or three different profiles for themselves."

I sat there trying to absorb all the other pertinent details Pam was telling me, especially when it came down to the fee structure. I couldn't help but wonder if I could do as well as Ling. I didn't want to get my hopes up too high, especially after the whole pot ordeal, but I couldn't help but feel excited over the prospect of possibly making $20,000 a month. A smile spread across my face and for the first time in many months, I allowed myself to feel slightly optimistic.

CHAPTER 14

꙰

MY BIG DILEMMA THAT WEEK was whether or not I was really going to tell Beaver about my new job. It wouldn't be too hard to keep my job a secret from Beaver with him working out of town and only coming home twice a month for a visit.

Pam did mention that the girls work only when they want to, so I can easily book the time off when Beaver is in town. He would never know.

I knew I ran the risk of having my new secret exposed if Beaver decided to break up with me and tell others. The best option would be to break up with him and not tell him about the escorting. But then I would look like a cold, heartless bitch after how supportive he'd been with the grow op. In the end, with any ounce of good moral I had left, I decided it would be best to tell Beaver the truth. He needed to make the decision to stay or leave. Because this was a conversation I didn't want to have over the phone, I decided to wait a few days until Beaver was back in town.

"Can we talk?" I asked him nervously one night.

"Sure. What's up?" He smiled showing off his unsightly teeth.

"Um… well, I don't know how to say this, so I'm just going to come out and tell you. You know I'm in a lot of debt right?"

"Yeah…," Beaver replied.

"Well, I decided to become an escort to try and pay off my debt," I blurted out.

"What!?" Beaver screeched, "Are you fuckin' serious!?"

"Yes. I've already gone and talked to an agency. They hired me on the spot."

"Of course they did. Look at you," Beaver interrupted.

"I've applied for an escorting license from the city. I should get it in a few days and then I can start working. I really don't know what else I can do that might make me quick cash to pay off my debt. The agency only has one Asian girl working there and she makes $20,000 cash a month working four days a week, so maybe I can make some decent money, too," I paused trying not to cry. "I don't know. I may not make much at all and end up quitting in a month but I've got to try."

"And you can't try by finding any other job. Anything but this?" Beaver asked, still upset.

"I can certainly work three or four jobs and never sleep. But the reality is it will take me forever to pay off my debt whereas I can try this escorting thing for a couple of months. And if it works out, then I can pay off my debt in no time. If it doesn't, then I can go and get three jobs," I replied, losing patience.

"Have you any idea what you'll have to do for that money?"

"Yes. I'm not dumb. It will involve sex and I'm prepared for that. It's my body and I can do as I please with it. I'm a grown ass woman making a grown ass decision!" I hollered defensively. "I don't want to justify my actions or decisions to you. I got myself in this mess and I need to do whatever it takes to get myself out. If you don't want to be with anymore, then I understand."

Beaver sat there quiet for a second before he let out a huge sigh. "Lina, you know I'm crazy about you. I can't just up and leave you and especially now. I'd be way too worried about you."

"Well, what are you going to do?" I asked, feeling slightly calmer.

"I don't know. I love you and I don't want to leave but at the same time the thought of some guy fucking my girl..." he said in an irate tone while pushing back his glasses.

"I know, but it's just a job. There's not going to be any emotions in it. It's just sex," I replied while trying to embrace Beaver. "How about we make up some ground rules?"

"I don't ever want to hear any details about your work," Beaver uttered furiously.

It was just like Beaver to avoid talking about things that were too hard for him to deal with. Beaver's emotional maturity was severely stunted after his mother's death. When topics became too hard for him to talk about he would either shut down completely or he would turn on his wry sense of humor and crack a joke to ease his discomfort. This suited me just fine. I was never one to discuss my traumas, so even though on the outside we were a mismatched pair, inside we were perfectly compatible.

"That works for me and listen, I'll always use protection and I'll get checked regularly. I don't want to catch anything and I don't want to give you anything."

"Well yeah… obviously…," Beaver replied sarcastically almost cracking a joke but then stopping.

"You are absolutely amazing and way too good to me," I said, leaning over and kissing him.

CHAPTER 15

ꝯb

WITH MY LICENSE IN MY hands, I went into the office to see Pam again. As I walked up the stairs to the office, I couldn't help but think how just two weeks ago I was running a full-fledged grow op in my basement. Now, I was going to be an escort. Things were happening at lightning speed and left me little time to process anything.

"Good," Pam beamed as I handed her my license. "I'll make you available for calls now." She busily sprayed herself with cheap perfume to mask the smell of a hundred cigarettes.

"Make sure the guy always gives you cash and at no time do you mention that the cash is in exchange for sex. Those undercover cops are always trying to bust new girls like yourself, so be careful what you say. Got it!?" Pam instructed.

"Yes," I nodded nervously.

"There's a fine line between escorting and prostitution. As an escort you're paid for your time, and quite frankly, I don't give a rat's ass what you choose to do in that time," Pam continued. She then pulled deodorant out of her purse and proceeded to cover her armpits in it.

Jeez. Heard of taking care of your personal hygiene at home?

"You'll need to go and get some pictures taken so we can put it on our web-site. One of the girls here is an amateur photographer. She can do it for you," Pam ordered.

"But I don't want my picture online. I don't want anyone to know what I'm doing."

"Don't worry. We'll block your face so no one will know. It'll be discreet," Pam assured.

"Okay, so what do I do now?" I asked innocently.

"Go home and I'll call you when there's a request."

I wasn't sure how long it would take for me to get my first call but I honestly thought if I was lucky Pam might call me in a week. Besides having my license, I wasn't set up for business. We were responsible for advertising our services in the newspaper at our own expense and I didn't have any money for it, so I opted to wait until I made some money. In addition, I didn't have any pictures online yet, so it came as a huge surprise when my phone rang two hours later for a "general call."

General calls were when guys would call in and didn't have a request for any particular girl. The calls would be prioritized to whichever girls were manning the phone and if it was Pam that was working she would give it to any girl she desired and luckily for me she took a liking to me.

"You've got your first call. The guy wants a petite girl. Do you want to take it?" Pam asked.

"Sure," I replied, shaking.

"Okay, remember to call me when you get there. That's really important. We want to make sure that all our girls are safe on their calls and this is how we track where you are."

I stared at the number Pam gave me for what seemed like ages before I snapped out of it.

Shit! It's really happening.

An hour later I pulled up to the hotel where the client instructed me to meet him. Even with the engine turned off, I was such a nervous wreck that I couldn't get out of the car.

What if he's undercover and I get busted? What if he's just so nasty I can't even take my clothes off? Remember this is just a job. This is just a fuckin' job! Just do it, get the money and get out. Don't put any emotions into it. Just breathe. Everything will be okay.

With Jell-O-like legs, I managed to find my way to his room. Then, I patiently waited for him to open the door for me.

It's not too late to back out. You can just turn around and drive home. The hell with all this. No, I'm fine. I can do this.

I was greeted by a clean-cut white guy in his early forties who was tall and lean with a good head of hair. By the look on his face, I was better looking than he anticipated.

"Boy, did I luck out today. Wow, you're beautiful!" he said, grinning from ear to ear. "I'm Daniel."

"I'm Lucy," I replied nervously. "How long would you like my company for?" I slowly asked as I tried to mask the fact that my entire body was shaking.

"I'll do an hour," Daniel replied nicely as he reached into his wallet and handed me the cash.

I pulled out my phone and called Pam. "Hi, I'm here with Daniel. He's booked me for an hour."

"Okay, good. I'll call you in forty-five minutes to tell you time's up. We never give those poor bastards a full hour," Pam chuckled as I hung up the phone.

"How long have you been doing this for?" Daniel asked.

"Oh, about a year now," I lied. I didn't want him to know that I was a rookie and I sure as hell didn't want him to know that he was my first.

"How do you like it?"

"It's pretty good. Pays my university tuition." I lied again.

"What are you studying?" Daniel continued.

"Business. I'm in my first year," I replied, continuing with my lie. His small chat was encouraged because I wanted to prolong doing the inevitable.

"Why don't you come and lie down on the bed?" Daniel directed.

Fuck! Here we go. Well, at least he's not fat and gross. Okay, I can do this.

He leaned in close and planted a wet slobbery kiss on my lips. It was an inexperienced kiss from a guy who looked like a computer geek and probably didn't get laid a whole lot. His tongue moved randomly in my mouth with no sense of direction. With an unexpected thrust, he had shoved it down my throat awakening my gag reflexes.

"Daniel that was great," I lied as I pushed him away from me. "I'm going to go freshen up for you. Why don't you just lay there and wait for me?"

"Okay Lucy. Hurry back," Daniel replied. He looked like he was ready to unleash his load.

I sat in the bathroom for a good ten minutes staring at the dark eyes that gazed back at me in the mirror. They say the eyes are the window to your soul and the eyes that were reflecting back at me were ones that were saddened and lost. The constant battle between light and dark... good and evil... morals and lack of morals teetered back and forth in my head.

You can do this, Lina. You can do this. Think about the money! This whole thing is a big mistake. Turn around and leave before it's too late! Yeah, well how are you going to pay off your debt? You have no education. You're nothing but a university dropout with big ambitions but no backbone to see things through. I thought you said you'd do anything to get out of debt. Well, this is anything. Go out and finish the job you were hired to do and stop acting like a pussy.

"Is everything okay in there?" Daniel yelled.

"Yeah, everything is fine," I replied wiping the tear that had fallen down my cheek.

In the end, the darkness had overtaken the light and I surrendered to the belittling voice inside of me. I left that bathroom arming myself with false confidence and pulled from my experience of wanting to become an actress as a pre-teen to parlay that into the role of a sexy vixen well enough to finish my job and leave the client thoroughly beaming.

Later on that evening, while soaking in the bath to cleanse myself of the filth I felt from my afternoon with Daniel, I decided that if I was going to continue in the business, then I needed to come up with boundaries to protect myself physically and emotionally. This included not offering any specialty services. Girls that offered specialties could charge a sizeable amount of money for their services, but this would involve playing into men's fantasies which can be anything from anal sex or bondage or the even more explicit fantasies of getting urinated or defecated on. Call me boring, but I wasn't willing to do anything other than the straight-laced act of vaginal sex. As much as money motivated me, I didn't want to do anything that made me feel even more degraded. In addition, I wasn't keen on Daniel kissing me, so I decided that there would be absolutely no exchange of bodily fluid that couldn't be protected by a condom. This meant kissing and oral copulation to be done on myself was off the table. I also knew if I was going to survive in this business, then I would have to protect my biggest asset which was my vagina and stick to a one fuck per booking limit. All these rules ran the possible risk of me not getting booked but I was determined to find another way of having my services deemed valuable to the client. The only problem was finding out what that was.

Now that I figured out my physical boundaries, I also needed to protect myself emotionally which meant I had to somehow totally disengage emotionally when with the client, all the while acting like I cared. It was something that was easier said than done but it was a skill I needed to master quickly in order to become successful. I knew this involved having to come up with a phony identity and even though I had already decided on the names of Lucy, Helena, and Asia, I still needed to complete it with a story.

I liked the storyline of the poor university student, escorting part-time to pay for her tuition. This set a precedent that I was somewhat intelligent and not escorting to support a drug habit. As well, I liked the idea of coming off as Chinese rather than Vietnamese because I found most of the time people couldn't really distinguish between the two and somehow hiding as a Chinese national made me feel safer from exposing my real identity.

By the time I stepped out of the bath I was feeling exhausted and ready for a good night's rest. However, my peaceful rest was interrupted shortly after by the annoying ring of my phone.

"There's a call requesting for an Asian girl. Do you want to take it?" a sweet voice bellowed.

This isn't Pam. Ah right; she only works during the days.

"Do I have to go right now or is he booking for another day?"

"Well, it's for right now. That's how it works," the girl responded in a very annoyed tone.

I somehow had it in my mind that bookings would be made in advance, like an appointment, and not on a whim. But I would learn quickly that I was literally on call from 7am-2am. No calls were ever booked in advance because it wasn't like these men knew when they were feeling frisky and needed company.

It was always of spontaneity which was something I loathed as I was one who embraced routine.

"Okay, give me his number," I replied, feeling agitated.

Getting out of bed at 12:30 in the morning wasn't at all appealing to me, but I needed the money. All sleepiness vanished when the client requested that I bring a few pairs of my dirty underwear.

What the fuck?! He wants me to bring dirty underwear? What the hell does he want me to do with my dirty underwear? Why are men so disgusting?

The hotel where I was to meet the client at was located not too far from where I grew up. It was where cheap hookers and crackheads hung out. And, here I was, about to walk in and fuck some strange guy who was most likely high out of his mind. The signs were all there for me just to go back to bed and forget about the call, but it's true what they say about being young and stupid. I ignored any instincts I had regarding my safety and found myself inside the filthy hotel lobby an hour later. Luckily for me, I was able to slip by the front desk undetected. I made my way into the rattling elevator and down an eerie half-lit hallway that bared resemblance to something out of a horror movie.

I knocked on the door and was greeted by a short, stocky white guy with a wife beater on. He must have been in his fifties with mid-length salt-and-pepper hair that was slicked back. He had a full moustache to match. As I stepped into the room, the fumes of his previously smoked ten cigarette butts hit my nostrils and made me dizzy. Since quitting smoking, I became very sensitive to second-hand smoke.

"I'm Bob," he said, introducing me in the same hoarse voice I heard on the phone.

"I'm Helena. It's nice to meet you. How long would you like me to stay?" I asked pleasantly.

"Well, I guess for the hour but I won't take that long."

Well, at least he's honest.

As Bob handed me the cash, I dialed the agency number and reported to them that I would be there for an hour.

"Well, you're a pretty girl," Bob continued. "Did you bring me what I asked for?"

"The dirty underwear? Yes, I brought three pairs," I replied as I reached into my purse and pulled them out.

Before I could even ask him what he needed them for he reached over and grabbed them from my hands, inhaling deeply as he held my unlaundered underwear to his nose.

Holy shit! What the fuck is wrong with this guy?

"Um, what would you like me to do?" I asked perplexed at what was happening.

"Nothing, sweetheart. Just sit there and watch me," he said, continuing to sniff as he slowly reached down and unzipped his pants to masturbate.

I sat there in bewilderment as I watched Bob jerk off to my stinky underwear. The whole situation was so bizarre and I didn't know whether to laugh or pretend to be turned on. I always heard about people having weird fetishes but I actually didn't think I would ever bear witness to any of it. Within minutes, Bob had unleashed his load and was reaching for a cigarette, leaving me still in disbelief as to what just went down.

"That was amazing. Thank you for doing this," he said as he exhaled his smoke.

For doing what? For bringing you some dirty underwear?

"No problem. Is that all you want from me?"

"Yeah, but if you don't mind, can I keep your underwear?"

Well, yeah... if you pay for them. I'm going to milk this weirdo for everything he's got.

"Sure, you can keep them but it's going to cost you."

"How much?"

"$100 a pair!"

"$100?!" Bob exclaimed.

"Yeah, unless you want to jerk off to your wife's dirty panties."

"No, I'd rather roll over dead five times than touch her dirty crotch."

Okay, and the guy is funny.

I let out a laugh which seemed to amuse Bob.

"Okay, I have $200 left in my wallet. Will you take that?"

"Sure," I responded as I grabbed the $200.

I can't believe this! $200 for three pairs of dirty underwear!

I walked out of the room still in awe that someone would pay that kind of money for rancid underwear. I could only wish that all my calls would be this easy. As I drove home, any uneasiness I may have felt with Daniel seemingly vanished as I calculated how much I'd made my first day as an escort.

Wow! I can't believe it! It's really not too bad.

CHAPTER 16

❦

A MONTH INTO ESCORTING, I would finally meet the infamous Candy. The girls in the agency liked to gossip and even though I tried my best to avoid any agency drama, I couldn't help but feel inquisitive about Candy—a transgender. Apparently, Candy was born a male and had gone back to Thailand to get a sex change to become a woman. Prior to her sex change she was working at the agency as a transvestite. So when I received a call from the agency telling me that a client had requested Candy and myself, I accepted the call out of sheer curiosity.

I showed up to a beautiful mansion in a very affluent part of the city. At the door, I was cheerfully greeted by Candy, a dark-skinned, slim girl with long, flowing black hair. I was discreetly trying to find any hints of her former male self but I couldn't. There were no traces of an Adam's apple and her features were soft and delicate, but the reality was she was very unattractive despite the heavy makeup she had on. The most attractive part about her was her huge breasts that sat on her petite frame.

Candy and I engaged in conversation with our older prominent client as he bragged about his newly divorced status and the successful business he owned. As Candy was attending to his every word and showering him with a ridiculous amount of affection, I was more enamored with Candy. I was riveted by the way she moved her body in beautiful feminine strides and the way she articulated her dainty girlish voice. I had been exposed to many gay people through Carmen, but up until now I'd never met someone who was transgender. I found it fascinating, but at the same time the situation felt a little awkward to me.

Before long we were headed to the client's bedroom to have that threesome he so much fantasized about with his requested "two exotic beautiful Asian girls."

If he only knew she used to be a man. I can't believe I'm about to do this.

We walked up the massive spiraling staircase into a grand master bedroom. It was impeccably furnished with a California king-size bed and a sitting area complete with a fireplace. A glimpse into his closest showed rows upon rows of expensive suits, and as I walked into the master bathroom to freshen up, I was surrounded in the opulence of European elegance.

Jeez, it's just ridiculous how rich some people are.

Back in the bedroom, Candy was already topless and making out with the client as I stood there, marveling in the robustness of her perfect breast implants.

Wow, she had a good surgeon!

I was pulled over by the client but as he tried to kiss me, I pulled away and killed the moment by going over my rules. He obviously didn't like how prude I was, so he reverted back to Candy who was more open to his requests. This served me well because I was content with having Candy do all the work. As he slowly peeled Candy's pants off, revealing a sexy red lace thong, I held my breath in anticipation of what I was about to see. Was there still going to be a little penis sticking out somewhere or was there going to be a large scar where they had cut off the penis? I was pleasantly surprised when he ripped off Candy's thong to reveal a normal looking vagina.

Holy shit! She really did have a great surgeon! You can't even tell.

Would it feel different from a real vagina? Would he be able to feel the difference between mine and hers? Apparently not because he was on her and in her in no time. Now this isn't the kind of threesome you see in porn that's all hot and heavy. It was plain awkward because Candy and my number one priority was to keep the sex as clean as possible. So, every time he switched back and forth between the two of us, we would have to wipe him clean and change condoms, making the whole act very robotic and so very unsexy.

I'm sure the client was feeling the same because halfway through he decided to stick with Candy while I lied there moaning, creating good sound effects to heighten the eroticism. Afterwards, the client requested that Candy stay longer, so I gathered my things and left. In all honesty, Candy was way more into it than I was and I was okay with having been outdone by her.

CHAPTER 17

༻

THREE MONTHS INTO ESCORTING AND what seemed like the biggest misfortune turned out to be the best thing to have happened for me. One Friday morning I received a frantic call from Pam.

"Listen... the agency got raided last night," Pam informed in a stressed out voice.

"What? What do you mean it got raided?" I asked.

"Yeah... this happens from time to time, but listen... don't worry too much. You don't last thirty years in the business without the best lawyer in town."

"Okay," I responded. "So what do we do in the meantime?" I was uncertain of what was to come.

"Just sit tight and don't say a word if the cops call."

"What do you mean if the cops call? They have my number?" I replied panicking.

"They took all the girls' info during the raid. But don't worry. Nothing's gonna happen," Pam said reassuringly as she hung up the phone.

Goddamn cops! What if they call and tell my family what I'm doing? Shit! What if they really shut down the agency? Where would I work? Just when I'm making good money, this happens!

All I knew was that I had to get my hands on the newspaper. When I did, the picture of our Madame was plastered on the front page. I read the article three times over trying to understand why the City legalized escorting, even going as far as licensing us for it, only to turn around and try to shut it down.

The article described our Madame as a ruthless woman running the largest escorting agency in the city that was a big cover-up for prostitution. They were determined to shut down the agency ASAP and put an end to the other numerous alleged illegal activities that were happening.

I couldn't have disagreed more with the article because the few times that I did meet our Madame, she was nothing but kind and gracious to me. But maybe that was because I was one of her top girls and she was making so much money from me. Still, I didn't mind the fees I had to pay because what Pam said was true: the agency never made you work or take a call if you didn't want to. You truly did everything at your own free will, very unlike the picture that the media painted. They described her as a forceful Madame that preyed on us innocent girls. The reality was the City knew exactly what we were up to and even licensing us to do it, only to turn around and sell it as groundbreaking news. What a bunch of hypocrites!

That evening I expected it to be quiet and it was. But true to Pam's word, the agency was up and running without the cops questioning a single one of us girls. Even so, Ling was so paranoid from the raid. She was afraid the cops might expose her to her family, so she quit. Overnight, I amassed all of Ling's clientele, making me the busiest girl in the agency. Being the top girl in the agency afforded me the opportunity to be especially selective of my clientele. I had paid my dues the first three months, but now it was all about to change. The ball was in my court now. And I was about to make some big changes.

The first thing I did was raise my rates which was gutsy, but I was determined to market myself as a high-end escort. Like any luxury product, I would come with a higher price point. I had already built up a handful of exclusive clientele for myself that fit the bill. All I needed to do now was screen all of Ling's clients. Screening clients was always the challenging part because it would happen over the phone. All I could go by was the way they spoke or by the address or hotel they were staying at which proved to be successful for the most part.

Even though my services came with so many limitations, I finally found the secret in making my services valuable to achieve client retention. As it turns out, I have the natural ability to read people and understand, in a short amount of time, what their needs are. Playing into these men's needs meant giving them the whole girlfriend experience. They didn't want to feel like a john; they were already so unhappily married at home that I didn't need to further disrespect them. I didn't want to make them feel ashamed for having to pay for sex.

The unhappy marriage experienced at home equaled a very sexless marriage, but repeatedly, I would hear from my wealthiest clients that it's easier to stay married than get a divorce. There was the handful of traveling executives who were away from home so often that they had urges that needed to be attended to. It's like an itch that can't be reached, and it needs to be scratched so badly that the only solution is to hire someone to do it. It didn't mean they didn't love their wives, but simply a difference in the wiring of men and women. Men are able to sleep with women to fulfill their animalistic nature without any emotional attachment.

Tanya often asked me how I so effortlessly played all these men. But it wasn't so much that I was playing them, it was more a keen awareness of their energy. Or, some may call it good instinct. I didn't know what to make of it because I wasn't trying to understand the embodiment of empathy. It was easier for me to rationalize it with my great acting skills that came from many years of classes when I was younger.

Besides, being empathetic meant that I cared about people. Even if this was truly what lied beneath my layers of scar tissue, I wanted to believe that being with these men, and dangling the sex in front of them like you would meat in front of a dog, presented me with a power that I never felt in my life. As twisted as the reasoning may sound, it made perfect sense to me and I bathed in the glory of it. I had never managed to be successful at anything I did in my life. But somehow, coming from a broken childhood made me so incredibly good at escorting and resulted in insurmountable success. After my first day, it was easy to bury any rage I felt under a huge pile of cash. I could easily convince myself that I was finally happy. And now with my debt paid off in just three months, I felt unstoppable.

CHAPTER 18

٩۶

AT LEAST HALF OF MY business came from four men, eventually earning them their own nicknames. All of them were so different from each other and I was their only commonality. I met Coin Boy one evening when I was called to his house and was greeted by a disheveled looking guy in his thirties.

"What's wrong?" I asked sympathetically, leaning in to stroke his dark luscious brown hair.

"Oh, it's nothing," Coin Boy replied, frowning.

"It's okay. You can tell me. It's not like we have the same friends that I would gossip this to," I coaxed as I continued to stroke is thick hair while snuggling next to him on the couch.

"Well…," Coin Boy continued hesitantly. "My wife came home last month and out of the blue she asks me for a divorce. I don't know what happened! I thought we were happy and now she tells me she wants the house and she's threatening me with my two little girls. She knows they mean everything to me."

"So what are you going to do?" I asked gently, sensing his vulnerability.

"I don't know. She can have the house. I don't care about that, but she can't have full custody of the girls. Those girls are my whole life," he replied with glistening eyes.

"And where are they now?" I asked uneasily. "You don't expect them home anytime soon, do you?"

"No, they're out of town visiting their grandparents for the weekend," he answered with great sadness.

Wow! I kind of feel sorry for this guy.

"I know you're going through a lot and I can't pretend to understand but I'm sure you called me here to momentarily forget about your troubles. Why don't you just try to forget about everything for the next hour and let's have some fun," I chirped, trying to get him out of his somber mood. "Or, I mean if you want, we can just talk. You can let everything out and that might make you feel better."

"No, you're right. Let's go to the bedroom," he responded as he guided me up the stairs.

Sitting on the edge of his bed embracing me, he asked shyly, "Is it okay if I undress you?"

"Sure," I whispered.

Wow! This is a nice guy.

Coin Boy slowly peeled off my dress, revealing one of my many sexy lingerie getups that I had invested in with my hard-earned cash.

"Wow, you're beautiful and your skin feels so soft," he spoke as he gently moved his hands up and down my back.

He held me in a tight embrace while lingering on my sweet scent and silky skin. As I reciprocated his motions, he closed his eyes, absorbing my touch as if this was the first time in a long time a woman had caressed him. He enjoyed the contact immeasurably and when it came time for the intimacy, he was so tender and caring. I thought maybe he was envisioning that I was his wife and he was making love to her. Not often are my clients that tame, so that made my experience with him so endearing and made me enjoy being around him that much more.

"Can you stay another hour?" he asked when he was done. "I just want to cuddle. I don't want to be alone." When he spoke, he exposed the acute pain he felt from his impending divorce.

"Absolutely," I answered as I lay in bed letting Coin Boy spoon me affectionately.

That first experience led to many more nights of Coin Boy crying on my shoulders. His marriage continued to crumble with the news of his wife leaving him for a wealthier man. It came as no surprise to me that she was basically upgrading her average husband to someone with better means.

Coin Boy was a decent man who was a hopeless romantic and what he was able to provide financially for his family was not enough for her. Even though the stories I heard were biased from his side, I couldn't help but relate to his wife because money equaled stability. No amount of love he had for his family was enough to make her feel secure, especially when his income fluctuated due to his job in the gaming industry.

Even in his financially strapping situation, he continued to see me, each time paying me with rolls upon rolls of coin. I found that odd at first, but then again money is money and I wasn't going to discriminate against coin or paper. It seemed the more turmoil he experienced from his looming divorce, the more he would reach out to me. I was part therapist and part escort. Every minute he spent with me was so valuable because it came at a huge cost for him with my hourly rate being way too expensive for him to afford, let alone my nightly rates.

I don't know if I just caught Coin Boy at a low point in his life where any kind of affection, whether genuine or not, was enough to console his longing to be loved. Out of all my clients, he needed the girlfriend experience to be legitimate in order to mend his broken heart and move on from his wife. For myself, I was simply exerting my professionalism. I gave him the most authentic girlfriend experience so that I could retain him as a client. However, I was so good at my job that Coin Boy believed that my services were our reality.

One afternoon while out shopping with Coin Boy, I was sifting through a row of dresses when he asked me the unimaginable.

"We've been seeing each other on a regular basis… and I don't know about you, but I want you to be my steady girlfriend," he said.

What the fuck?!

I should have seen this coming but I wanted to believe that he was intelligent enough to differentiate between truth and reality. The truth is: you fuck escorts, not fall in love with them. I knew that I had let him stretch my time a little too far with our frequent shopping sprees. Coin Boy preferred to take me shopping because it enabled us to act more like a couple. In all honesty, I would rather have the cash. Being seen in public with him ran the possibility of having my real identity exposed. But I was still being nicely compensated for my time, so I let it slide… and now I was in a situation that left me completely shell-shocked in response.

"Um… I don't think this is the right time to talk about this," I replied, trying to stay as calm as possible. "What do you think of this dress?" I asked, trying to change the topic.

"It's nice. Can we talk about this later?" Coin Boy asked. "Can I take you out to dinner tonight?"

"I'm busy tonight. I thought we were just shopping today until 5:00," I responded in quiet frustration, knowing that every minute of my time mattered.

"Yes, but I really want to talk to you about us. I've been thinking about it a lot lately. When can I have dinner with you? I don't want to keep paying every time I want to see you."

Oh God!

"Okay, maybe we can leave here a little earlier and we can go for dinner. But we have to be done by 6:00, okay?"

"Okay!" Coin Boy replied.

A couple thousand dollars' worth of new clothing later, we were cozied up side by side in a booth.

Jeez… this is just too much!

Before we even had a chance to order our food, Coin Boy turned to me and said, "Laina" That's right. He even had a nickname for me. Although I went by the name Helena with him, he thought it would be cute to shorten it to Laina. "I really, really like you. I'm completely falling for you. I just can't help it."

Oh brother!

With a deep breath I turned to face Coin Boy and while holding his hands, I responded, "You can't possibly be falling for me. I'm just an escort. You deserve better than me," I told him.

"That's the thing. I don't care that you're an escort. I like you for you. I don't care what you do for work."

You don't even know who I really am. You love the person I created for you. You don't even know about Beaver.

"I don't know about this. If we're serious, then you'll make me quit my job and I need my job to pay for school and rent," I replied.

"No, I won't make you quit your job. You can keep working. Or, if you don't want to, then I can take care of you and I'll pay for everything. How much do you even make anyways? I'm sure I can cover it. I've basically been taking care of you since we've met," Coin Boy continued as he let out a chuckle.

Wow, are you fuckin' serious?! I make more money than I know what to do with.

"I don't know," I replied reluctantly. "I'm really independent and I don't want anyone taking care of my bills for me. Besides, how are you going to handle it when I have to leave you and go meet another client?"

"I'll be okay, Laina. I'm not a jealous person. Besides, I know it's just your job and as long as you say we're together, then that's all that matters."

I sat there in silence wondering how I would break it to him that I was happy with things exactly the way they were.

"How about we go on a little trip?" Coin Boy asked.

"What kind of trip?" I replied curiously.

"Well, I have to go to Vancouver in two weeks for some business. Why don't you come out and join me?"

"How is this going to work? Do you want to book me for a day or how many days do you want to book me for? You know you can't afford my overnight rate."

"This is what I mean!" Coin Boy said raising his voice. "I don't want to book you. I just want you to come as my girlfriend and spend some time with me. I'll pay for your airfare.... hotel.... everything. I'll take you shopping and we can have all kinds of fun. I just don't want to deal with paying you every time I see you. You know you're a very expensive girl!"

"Well, I never agreed to be your girlfriend," I replied. "You knew exactly what you were getting into when you started using my services. Now all of a sudden you want to change things and I'm supposed to agree to it right away? I need some time to think things over. Listen, I'm going to go home and think about things."

"But we haven't even eaten yet."

"I'm not hungry anymore."

"Laina, I'm so sorry I upset you. Don't be like this."

"No, I have to go."

"Well, when will I see you again?"

"Whenever you want. Just call the agency."

I left Coin Boy sitting at the restaurant looking glum. I was dismayed by how the situation unfolded and how I was going to handle it.

CHAPTER 19

✑

ONE AFTERNOON, I ACCEPTED A call to meet a new client at a mediocre hotel. That was where I met Rock Boy—who initially came across as very unassuming. For a fifty-year-old who was experiencing great hair loss, he was able to maintain great physical shape which explained his stamina in bed. Initially, Rock Boy's cold demeanor gave me the impression that he wasn't really into me. However, my charm eventually wore off on him when I had him believe that I was a university student working towards a business degree after he revealed his impressive academe. From there, I continued seeing him multiple times a week with him often changing hotels because of his ultra-paranoia that his wife would discover his double life.

The more I saw Rock Boy, the more I disliked him because of the way he made me feel which was that of a cheap whore. I detested the way he spanked or barked commands at me. Not being able to manipulate the client the way I was used to invoked a lack of control. When I feel like I have control of the situation, then the money doesn't come covered in filth whereas money earned in great submission comes with guilt knowing that I would allow another human being to degrade me.

I endured our time together because, although he carried a bold arrogance, at times I saw slivers of a considerate person. It made me question if we were more similar than different. Could it be possible that underneath that rock-like persona was a kind person who was also deeply wounded along the way? His confused actions that faltered between domineering fornication and courteous conversing led me to believe he was a very complicated individual.

Perhaps internally, Rock Boy was intricately woven. But externally, he was anything but. I must have seen him a dozen times and every single time he would wear the exact same variation of clothing which consisted of blue denims, a sweater and brown loafers. I was perplexed as to why someone who owned their own company and bolstered to be worth millions would dress so shabby.

One afternoon, after a sexually charged escapade that ended with him slapping my ass so hard it sent waves of pain up my spine, Rock Boy collapsed on the bed. Between heavy breathing he asked, "Have you ever been to London?"

"Like London, England?" I asked while soothing the pain from my ass.

"Yes, London, England," Rock Boy replied slightly annoyed.

"No, I've never been anywhere in Europe but I'd love to go one day."

"Well, would you like to go with me?"

Holy shit! Did he just ask me to go to London?

"Seriously?! When?" I asked, already forgetting about the ass slap.

"Well, I'm going to be in Europe for business in the fall. I was going to take a detour and go to London to visit some friends. If you want to join me, then we can stay for a week."

Oh my God! That's so exotic. But am I getting paid for this?

Rock Boy must have read my mind.

"I'll pay for the entire trip," he said. "Your airfare, hotel, food and whatever your daily rate is."

I didn't even know how much to charge him as no other client has ever asked me to accompany them on a trip. I mean, Coin Boy wanted to go on a trip with me but it wasn't at this caliber. The thought of going to London excited me dearly, but the notion of spending an entire week with him was unappealing. It was one thing to put up with him for a few hours a week but the idea of an entire week with anyone was hard to swallow. What wasn't hard to swallow was how Rock Boy, without any hesitation, agreed to the five figure fee that I blurted out.

"How would you like me to pay you? Can I write you a check?" Rock Boy asked promptly which reminded me that I liked how forthright he was when it came to money.

"No, cash is fine," I replied smiling.

"Okay, we'll meet up before I leave and I'll give you fifty percent up front and then when you get to London I'll pay you the remaining fifty. You can also book your own plane ticket and I'll reimburse you. Is that fair?"

"That sounds good," I answered, trying to contain my excitement.

I can't believe this. I'm going to London!

I was on cloud nine while driving home. I still couldn't believe that I was propositioned for an all-expense-paid trip overseas. Prior to this, I'd only really traveled domestically and a destination like Europe was so alluring it blocked all thoughts of aversion towards Rock Boy out of my mind, making me convince myself that I could muster up my best acting chops to withstand a week with him. After all, he was paying a premium for my services, so I would have to deliver a stellar performance.

CHAPTER 20

❦

ON MY WAY TO MEETING Lover Boy, I wondered if the lovely, polite, ever-so-sexy voice of the guy I just spoke with would match that of an attractive person. I seldom did that because rarely did I ever find my clients handsome. Pondering over what they may look like would almost always disappoint—most of the time I would have to conjure a better looking face in order to engage in sexual activities with them. To my delight, I was welcomed by a middle-aged man with salt-and-pepper wavy hair and intense blue eyes. He wasn't hot *per se* but it was his sultry voice and sleek clothes that I found, so sexy.

I was instructed to sit down in the sitting area of the big fancy suite that Lover Boy was staying in. As he sat down on the chair across from me, his bright eyes pierced into mine which made me rather uncomfortable as I found most people never really stared into anyone's eyes the way he was looking at mine.

"Tell me your story, Lucy," he questioned seductively.

Okay, this is weird. No one's really asked me that.

As I regurgitated my made-up character, Lover Boy listened like he was indeed interested. In return, he was not shy to share the fact that he was newly divorced. Before long, an hour flew by without me realizing that I never stopped once to anticipate how much time was left before I could leave.

"Lucy, I haven't eaten dinner yet. Would you like to stay and have dinner with me? We can order some room service," Lover Boy politely asked.

"That would be great. I haven't had dinner yet either."

Wow, I kinda like this guy.

By the time dinner arrived, Lover Boy looked up and inquired, "Would you like to stay the night with me?"

"Of course!" I responded trying to conceal my enthusiasm over the fact that overnight bookings rarely happened, not to mention the sizeable fee that I charged for it.

Oh my God! I can't believe my luck!

After a delicious dinner, I relaxed in the soaker tub of the luxury suite while Lover Boy treated me to an amazing scalp massage finished off with him washing every inch of my body.

Is this for real? I can't believe he's paying to make ME feel, so good.

After the bath, Lover Boy continued pleasing me with a full body massage. As I closed my eyes, for the first time since working in the industry, I forgot that I was an escort. His touch made me feel human and, in so doing, nourished me in a much-needed way. In a profession where I'm the one constantly giving and pleasing, to have the feeling reciprocated but, more importantly, allowing myself the ability to enjoy it created a profound intimacy. In deep relaxation, I felt a foreign tingling and looked up to see Lover Boy sucking on my toes. I'd never experienced such a sensation and even though my body enjoyed it, my brain was trying to analyze.

"Relax. Calm down. Close your eyes and let your body feel it," Lover Boy whispered.

It took every ounce of self-control not to break any of my rules with him that evening. He was an incredible lover who performed with just the right amount of tenderness coupled with equal amounts of assertion. Along the way he made sure to check in to see if I was okay. And I was more than okay because I truly enjoyed being with him which amazed me. After readily lavishing in the riches of the experience that Lover Boy provided, when both our bodies were saturated in satisfaction, he affectionately rolled over and spooned me as I fell asleep in his arms.

What happened that evening parlayed into many more nights that I would spend with Lover Boy at his new bachelor pad. Each time, I was paid tremendous amounts of money for him to please me.

"What are you doing tomorrow?" Lover Boy asked as we cuddled in bed.

"Nothing. I have no plans yet. What did you have in mind?" I responded.

"Well, I thought I would surprise you. I booked us in for an entire day at a spa!"

This was typical behavior from Lover Boy. He was a spontaneous guy and, luckily, being single and having no children afforded him this virtue.

"Are you serious?" I asked in shock. Even though I loathed surprises because that meant that it would take away from my carefully planned and regimented life, it was still an invited surprise.

"Yes! Absolutely."

"That is so awesome!" I screamed in joy. "What did you book us in for?"

"Well, nothing but the best for my Lucy. We are booked in for a full-day package. Manicure, pedicure, massage, facial, and a lunch in between. Plus, we can indulge in all the amenities."

"Wow! When did you plan all this? I can't believe it!"

"Last week. I wanted to do something special for you. You're such a special girl and you deserve to be treated like a princess," he beamed.

"I sure do!" I replied jokingly.

"You know Lucy, I don't know what's happening but every time I'm with you, it makes me so happy."

"Me too. I love seeing you," I replied truthfully. "How is this going to work?" I asked, quickly changing the topic as I sensed Lover Boy was trying to have a serious conversation with me.

"What do you mean?"

"Well, I'm assuming you want to book me for the entire day tomorrow if we're going to the spa. You know that my rates aren't cheap. Are you okay with it?"

"Oh Lucy, you're expensive but worth every penny," he remarked. "Stay the night and then we'll go to the spa tomorrow."

The spa we were going to was located ninety minutes outside of the city in a nearby resort town. Sitting in his convertible Porsche and breathing in the warm mountain air while admiring the scenery made me question whether or not I was really falling for Lover Boy. Being with him didn't feel like work. It felt effortless, and with the way things were unfolding it blurred all the lines, making it difficult for me to distinguish fact from fiction. I found him attractive in that he personified both masculine and feminine energy. His penchant for thrill-seeking activities such as bungee jumping or sky-diving balanced his nurturing affinity. In a nutshell he seemed almost too perfect to be true.

As we arrived at the spa it was nothing short of spectacular with its indoor and outdoor pools, hot/cold plunges and relaxation areas that give you premium views of nature. As we frolicked in the outdoor pool awaiting our couple's massage a nice elderly lady said, "It's nice to see a couple so in love."

I blushed as Lover Boy put his arms around me grinning as if I was really his. The whole day passed by too quickly and was everything you'd expect from an award-winning spa. By the end of the day, I was thoroughly relaxed as we held hands the entire drive home.

CHAPTER 21

ℭ

IF COIN BOY WAS THE one who always wore his emotions on his sleeve and epitomized what a hopeless romantic is, Rock Boy landed on the other end of the spectrum for being guarded and icy. Lover Boy was somewhere in the middle with his super suave and almost playboy-like attributes when it came to treating women. Then there was GQ Boy who exemplified a combination of all of them.

My first meeting with GQ Boy came late one evening when I was summoned to meet him at his office. Upon stepping into his office, I knew immediately that I was dealing with a high-power executive. His office was the big corner office on one of the top floors with sweeping views of the city that also accommodated a large sitting area and its very own full bathroom. Even though I would only frequent his office in the evenings when everyone was gone, it made our rendezvous much easier having access to your own private bathroom.

GQ Boy came across as all business in the best possible way by his impeccable taste in designer suits that he always wore. They were the best money could afford. Even though he was of smaller stature, the custom-made suits he wore elevated his height just enough that he seemed more intimidating on initial contact. Upon meeting, GQ Boy possessed a certain quietness, always listening more than talking—like a predator patiently watching its prey for the opportune time to attack. It wasn't done in a presumptuous nature but rather a bashful manner which I found endearing. I always talked way too much and therefore preferred that guys listened more than talked.

I had a profound appreciation for his rags-to-riches story. It made me respect him hugely because in his story I found commonality with my own.

I related to his poor upbringing and his desire to make something of himself with just a simple college certificate and sheer tenacity. I felt like I was the twenty-five years' younger female version of him because I possessed the same determination. GQ Boy was proof that if I worked hard enough, then all things are possible. I didn't have the same regard for the other three guys. Coin Boy's energy was too desperate and Rock Boy's university credentials were too intimidating. Even though I was most physically attracted to Lover Boy and I did indeed like him, liking someone and respecting someone are two different things.

Most of our encounters happened in his office. But on a few occasions GQ Boy would request that I escort him to some corporate functions. One of them happened to be on New Year's Eve. It was freezing out that evening but I still wanted to dress to impress, especially when I was going to be in a room surrounded by stuffy rich people. I slipped on a short sexy black dress with sky-high stilettos and even got my hair and make-up professionally done for the evening. So when GQ Boy and I arrived at the upscale restaurant all eyes were on the distinguished older gentleman and his arm candy date.

"Did I tell you how beautiful you look tonight?" GQ Boy whispered in my ear as he took off my coat and gave it to the hostess to coat check.

Yeah, like five times!

"Thanks. You don't look too bad yourself," I replied admiring his Armani suit.

The restaurant was packed full of people who were already rocking out to the live jazz band while sipping on cocktails. GQ Boy grabbed my hand and like the gentleman that he is walked us to our table and pulled my chair out for me while I got settled in. I recognized the other three men that were seated at our table from a previous event that I attended with GQ Boy. This time they had their wives with them which made me feel slightly uncomfortable.

"Don't worry. They won't bite," GQ Boy teased, sensing my discomfort.

Please don't let me run into anyone I know.

"I'm fine," I lied as I glanced around.

"Darling, whatever you're doing keep on doing it. I haven't seen him this happy in a long time," the glamorous woman seated across from me said.

"I think you need to take it easy with the wine," the man seated next to her chimed in.

"What? I'm just saying… he looks happy," she rebutted.

"Yes, things are good," GQ Boy acknowledged, placing his hand on my leg to reassure me that everything was okay.

I appreciated the small gestures GQ Boy made towards me in situations like this. It showed that he cared about my well-being. I didn't blame the curiosity his business associates had. After all, I seemingly appeared out of nowhere since his separation from his wife and now he was parading around with a girl half his age. Personally I would have much rather spent the evening in his office because being out in public with my clients always made me feel nervous. I couldn't refuse the big paycheck that came along with these functions, so I always tried my best to fit in. But it was always hard because most of the people were my parents' age.

More wine and cocktails flowed around our table. By the time we finished dinner everyone was on their way to drunk and any awkwardness initially felt had vanished. Tonight the roles were reversed and I found myself the quiet predator keeping a close eye on all my prey because I was the only sober one. I'd never been a big drinker, so the decision to give up drinking came easily. I didn't like the lack of control I felt when I was intoxicated. And I never really liked the taste of alcohol. More importantly, I hated what alcohol turned my father into and how it tore my family apart.

Watching GQ Boy interact when intoxicated was amusing. His usually reserved self was replaced with a more open and goofy attitude. He would laugh at his own jokes with a loud boisterous shriek that was infectious. Our company turned out to be a classy bunch because no one bragged about their riches. Instead, they focused on light conversations that didn't evolve around the economy and stocks.

"Come and dance with me," I insisted to GQ Boy.

"I'm warning you. I'm not much of a dancer," he replied.

"That's okay. I just want you all to myself for a while," I replied, pulling him up from his chair.

As we danced into the New Year, GQ Boy maintained his chivalry and always ensured that my comfort was his main priority. That made him so sexy in my eyes because here I was a twenty-four-year-old girl having an influential business exec eat out of the palm of my hand. That evening, even in his tipsy state, he sexed me tenderly as he usually does, which makes that part of my job a little more tolerable.

CHAPTER 22

꙳

I HADN'T SEEN TANYA IN months and our polar opposite work schedules allowed only the occasional phone calls. So, I was ecstatic when she was back in town for a few days to visit. We decided to have lunch at a nearby restaurant and as we settled into a booth, I couldn't help but notice how haggard Tanya was looking.

"Well, you look great!" Tanya complimented.

"Thanks. Are you okay? You look tired," I asked, concerned.

"I'm exhausted. I'm doing back-breaking labor and I just need to catch a break," she replied in a drained voice.

"How are things financially? Have you been able to pay off some debt?"

"Some, but not all. I need to do something else. Listen girl, I was thinking of quitting my job and escorting like you. What do you think?" Tanya questioned.

"Are you serious?" I asked, rather surprised.

"Yes. I'm sick and tired of what I'm doing… and for what? To make what you make in an hour!"

What the fuck. She can't do what I do. This is like stepping on my turf!

Tanya sensed my uncertainty, so she quickly continued, "I'll join a different agency so we won't be competing with each other."

"It's not about us competing with each other. I know you so well and I don't think you would be able to handle it. I literally think you would either throw up or punch these guys out. Sometimes you get good ones and sometimes there's bad ones," I replied agitated.

My agitation was a natural reaction to the insecurities that loomed inside me. In the years that I've known Tanya, she managed to outgrow her tomboy phase and turn into a classic beauty. What she also possessed that I didn't at the time was that she was an incredibly nice person and even though there was a good person inside of me somewhere, I just couldn't resurrect it. But my weakness was what became my strength in escorting. Tanya's strength would be somewhat detrimental.

"Well, if you can do it, then I think I can manage," Tanya replied defensively.

"Yes, but that's because I can fuck guys and have absolutely no feeling about it. You can't do that," I replied, raising my voice.

"Well, it doesn't seem that bad. All these guys are taking you on trips and shopping sprees. They treat you well," Tanya responded.

"That's only a very small percentage and you would have to know how to work them. It's something I can't teach you. You either have it or you don't. And this business can burn you out quickly. I'm exhausted every single day."

"Well, it hasn't been a walk in the park for me either. You don't think working sixteen-hour days makes you exhausted? Trust me, I think I'd rather do what you're doing. Besides, it didn't take you too long to land those four clients… your VIPs that spend thousands on you every month."

"You think this is easy but that's because I tell you all the good stories. I haven't told you stories of all the nasty calls I've been on!" I shouted angrily.

"It can't be that bad. I think you're just scared because you think I'm going to steal your business!" Tanya argued back.

"Well, yes… a part of me does think that, but the bigger part of me knows that there is no way you can emotionally deal with this shit!"

"Well, tell me some of your worst calls."

"Well, I've had plenty. I don't even know where to start. There was the time when I was called to a motel and when I walked into the room there was a ninety-year-old man in a wheelchair with an oxygen tube in his nose. He could barely even open the door for me. I swear he was going to croak right in front of me and even on his death bed he still wanted one last fuck! I couldn't do it. I took his money and left. He didn't even have the energy or strength to do anything about it."

"Wow! Ninety years old!" Tanya exclaimed in disbelief.

"Well, then there was the 500-pound obese guy. I don't know what was worse, the obese guy or the old fart! He was a young guy but he was so fat that he could barely walk to his room and then when he finally got to his bed, he needed another five minutes just to catch his breath. He asked me to take his sweat pants off for him and when I did all the fat rolls literally made my stomach sick. I just apologized to him and said I couldn't do it. But the thing was he was really nice and said he understood because this had happened before to him when he called another girl and he was hoping this time it would be different. When he said that, I felt so bad that I gave him a pity hand job which was the only thing I could stomach to do."

"Wow," Tanya said, shaking her head in disbelief. "How come you never told me these stories before?"

"Well, why would I? They're rather gross. I only wanted to share good parts about my job with you."

"Is that all or is there more?"

"Oh my God, there's so much more. There was the one guy who was physically handicapped. He had some kind of disease and both his legs were all mangled up. He was walking with a walker to open the door for me. I wasn't sure if I could go through with it, but I tried my best. I couldn't watch him undress, so I pretended to go to the washroom to freshen up. When I came out he was lying underneath the sheets. I was in my bra and panties and I knew the only way to fuck him was to ride him, so I got on top and the minute I did I got so freaked out by his legs that I had to leave."

"Then there was a guy who fantasized about sleeping with his daughter," I continued. "In fact, he told me that he had taken his daughter's virginity. She apparently had allowed him to do so, which I highly doubt, but since that day he hasn't touched her and he wanted to so badly. He asked me to role-play and pretend to be his daughter and call him Daddy in his native language. I can't remember what the fuck it was, but the whole time I was thinking how utterly disgusting this guy was to take his own daughter's virginity."

"Holy shit! That's so messed up!" Tanya proclaimed.

"I know… is this something you really want to do? If you think you can handle it, then go ahead. But as your best friend who knows you so well, I'm just trying to do you a favor by telling you straight out that this industry is not for you."

"It seemed so easy that I thought I could give it a try… but after hearing this, I don't know," Tanya hesitated.

"It is in a sense that I'm not sitting in an office being hounded by a boss. But it isn't because you're exposed to a lot of fucked up things and the bottom line is… can you really prostitute yourself out for money? Do you love money that much? Prostitution has always been a moral issue and will always be. Morally I couldn't give a fuck. I just count dollars while it's happening, but can you do the same?"

"No, I don't think I could."

"So that's what I'm trying to tell you. Not everyone could. Sometimes I think I'm just as fucked up as all these guys who call escorts because I can do it without so much as thinking about it, but I know you can't. It would eat you up inside."

"Well, I just heard all these stories about Coin Boy, Lover Boy, Rock Boy and what's the other one?" Tanya asked.

"GQ Boy."

"Yeah, GQ Boy, so I thought it was all like that."

"No, it's not all like that. Like I said, you have to build that type of clientele."

"But how did you get those clients? I'm sure all those girls in your agency would love to get the clients you book."

"To be honest, I really don't know. I guess I just lucked out."

"You've always been lucky."

"Not with growing pot," I laughed.

"Yeah, but it seems like you've always been lucky with men."

"No, I'm not lucky with men. I just know how to play the game. I've been hurt one too many times and unlike you, I learn from it. Listen… if you really want to become an escort, then do it. But don't say I didn't warn you."

"After hearing all your horror stories, I don't know if I could do it," Tanya replied.

The tension that was previously hanging between us evaporated as we enjoyed the remainder of our lunch together.

CHAPTER 23

∞

I TOOK COIN BOY UP on his offer and joined him in Vancouver for the day. Even though Coin Boy could only afford to pay half my day rate, the added perks of shopping and all my expenses covered was enough motivation for me to go. I also wanted to take the opportunity to respond to Coin Boy's proposition of a possible relationship between us, so on the airplane I went over what I was going to tell Coin Boy. I decided to agree on being his girlfriend as long as it didn't interfere with my work. The terms of the agreement were for him to pay for my tuition, which really didn't exist because I wasn't in school, and all my living expenses. I inflated the amount so that it worked out that I would get more from the monthly lump sum payment than from him paying me hourly. To ensure that he would be satisfied with the arrangement, I would throw in the occasional sleepovers to make our relationship more genuine. I viewed this as a game of chess and as long as I could keep the money coming in from him then it really was 'checkmate.'

I was making my way through the crowd at the Vancouver airport when I spotted Coin Boy frantically waving at me. As I ran towards him, he embraced me with a long hug.

"Oh Laina, I missed you so much!" he exclaimed.

"I missed you too!" I replied, trying to sound just as excited.

"How was the flight here?"

"It was good. I slept the whole way."

"Are you hungry?" he asked.

"Yes, I'm starving," I replied. "How about you?"

"I'm pretty hungry too, but can we check into our hotel first and then go grab a bite to eat?"

"Sure."

Coin Boy booked a hotel on a busy shopping street which worked out perfectly since I did plan on taking advantage of the shopping spree. The hotel wasn't anything spectacular, but it didn't really matter to me because I wasn't spending the night and whatever he could save on hotel meant he would spend on me. The minute we walked in the room, he lifted me up on his shoulder.

"Put me down!" I giggled as he walked over to the bed.

He dropped me on the bed and pinned himself on top of me.

Fuck, this already?

By the look on his face I could tell he needed it bad and I knew I couldn't wiggle my way out of this one. So I played into his fantasy and built up his ego with preposterous compliments that would make any average guy seem like Superman. I made sure to moan extra loud so that anybody walking by in the hallway could hear how this beefcake was rocking my world, and that indeed made him feel that much manlier.

"Laina, you drive me fuckin' crazy," he said breathlessly when he finished. "So have you thought about what I asked you?"

"Yes I have," I replied.

"You did?!" he exclaimed with a look of surprise on his face. "Well...?"

"Well, I thought about it and I think we can try it out, so long as you don't interfere with my work because you said that I don't have to quit my job."

"Yes, that's right. You don't have to quit your job," he replied, grinning from ear to ear.

"You have to give me my space. You know I don't have a lot of time with school and all."

"I understand," he nodded.

"And you agree to take care of all my schooling for me and cover my living expenses so that I don't have to work too much."

"Right," he nodded again.

So when I ran the numbers by him as to how much was adequate for me to survive it was met with a response of, "What?! Laina, that's a lot of money.

That's more than I thought it would be. You know I'm not rich, but if I was I'd give it all to you."

"I know, but that's how much it costs me for school and to live. My tuition and books keep going up and my landlord just raised my rent again," I lied, with an absolute straight look on my face.

Boy, I'm fuckin' good at this!!!

"I mean, you can give me less but that would mean less time with you."

"Okay, okay. I'll make it work even if I have to work two jobs. But you know I still have to pay my ex-wife child support."

"I know, but this is what you wanted. You asked for this. We can always go back to the way it was and you can just pay me hourly every time you want to see me."

"I don't want it like that. I want you to be with me and to be committed to me. I fuckin' love you, Laina! Can't you see that?"

Holy shit! Did he just drop the 'L' word on me?!!!

"Well, I'm falling hard for you too!" I lied.

"You are?" Coin Boy replied in astonishment.

"Yes. It's just that I'm different from you. I'm used to keeping my feelings inside."

"Well Laina, you can tell me these things, we're together now. I want you to tell me how you feel about me because sometimes I'm not sure if you really like me or if it's just about the money."

Oh my God. He's so stupid!

"Of course I like you or why else would I keep seeing you? Sometimes I feel like you put so much pressure on me," I lied while mustering up fake tears.

"Oh Laina. Don't cry," he said, rubbing my back and trying to sooth me. "I'm sorry. You're right. Maybe I do ask a lot from you but that's because I love you so much."

I can't believe he's falling for all this shit.

"Don't cry anymore. Let's go eat and I'll take you shopping," Coin Boy consoled.

"Okay," I replied as I wiped the fake tears away from my face.

Fuck! I should win an Academy Award for that performance!

We took advantage of the beautiful sunny day and as we made our way around downtown Vancouver, I made sure to be extra affectionate with him by turning on the PDA so that it was evident that I was his girl. He held my hand proudly and even though I was never keen on showing PDA with Beaver, I knew that Coin Boy needed the affection to validate his worth as a provider and man. Unbeknownst to him, his divorce and how his marriage ended wounded his ego and shattered his already-low self-esteem. I should have felt guilty for taking advantage of him but I was too self-absorbed to stop what I was doing. All I could do was justify it with the notion that he knew what he was getting into and it wasn't my responsibility to protect him.

Ever the gentleman, Coin Boy made sure to carry all my shopping bags and once we were done with lunch and shopping we made our way through Stanley Park like two lovebirds. He laid his jacket down for me to sit on while we took in the picturesque view of the water and seagulls.

As he stroked my long black hair, Coin Boy murmured, "I have a surprise for you."

Oh God. Don't tell me he's proposing.

"What is it?" I inquired. "You know I hate surprises."

"I know, but I couldn't help it. I bought you something," Coin Boy expressed as he reached into his backpack and pulled out two nicely wrapped boxes.

"Wow, thanks. Can I open it now?"

"Of course!" Coin Boy replied, anticipating my reaction to the gifts.

I ripped open the smaller gift and pulled out a beautiful delicate gold necklace.

"You shouldn't have... this must have cost you a fortune," I said in awe while admiring the diamond pendant that was hanging from the necklace.

"It did, but you're worth it. I saw it and immediately thought of you. It's so dainty and precious – just like you," Coin Boy beamed. "Now open your second gift."

The larger box contained a brand new cell phone.

"I bought it for you so that I don't have to call the agency when I need to reach you. Now I can call you directly," he smiled.

"Oh... well, thanks," I commented.

"Do you not like the phone? I can always go and return it for another one."

Of course I don't like the phone. This is going to be a pain in the ass for me.

"No... no... I like the phone. I'm just overwhelmed by the gifts. It's perfect. The whole day is perfect. Thank you," I replied in a phony tone.

"I know. I wish every day could be like today," he said as he affectionately caressed me. "Too bad you couldn't stay longer with me here," Coin Boy pouted.

"I know, but I'll see you when you get back."

"I love you, Laina," he whispered in my ears as I reached up to hug him.

"Thank you," was all I could muster up.

"You don't have to tell me you love me until you mean it but I need to express to you how I feel," Coin Boy said quietly.

I had to acknowledge that he was an unbelievable kind guy, but were his sweet actions enough for me to give up everything I'd worked so hard for... just so we can try to build a relationship on a make-believe foundation? It was impossible for me to open up my heart to anybody because even if I wanted to I just didn't know how.

CHAPTER 24

❧

"Lucy!" Lover Boy greeted enthusiastically as he hugged me at the door.

His ravenous eyes sent alerts that he needed me bad and it wasn't going to be a dinner and cuddles night as I hoped. As he guided me to his room and proceeded to slowly undress me, I stood there welcoming his touch.

Revealing my flat stomach and small breasts, Lover Boy breathed in the scent of my skin. "Wow... beautiful. Absolutely stunning!" he said, marveling at it all. I wasn't sure if it was my body he was complimenting me on or my new purple bra and panties that Coin Boy had bought me.

"The lingerie or the body?" I asked seductively.

"Both!" he exclaimed as he pressed his face in my abdomen and kissed it all over, sending shivers up my spine.

I couldn't restrain myself from the pleasures he was offering because with Lover Boy our sexual chemistry was undeniable. Still I assembled any willpower I had to stop him from giving me any oral ecstasy.

"You know you can't go there," I whispered in arousal.

"I know but can I just this once?" he pleaded as he continued to kiss the inside of my thighs until he came closer and closer to what I had denied him to do since we first met.

My body begged for the gratification but my mind was relentlessly denying it.

Don't let him do it. Fight it. You're here to do a job not to enjoy the job. Keep it separate. Keep it separate.

"No you can't. You know my rules."

"I don't like your rules," he whispered back while continuing to kiss all around the area.

"I know, but I need you to respect them," I strongly pleaded.

Knowing that I was slowly losing control of the situation, I quickly turned it around and opted to please him as he lay back and closed his eyes to the full enjoyment of my lips on his penis.

Yes. This is the way it's supposed to be.

I was in control again. That meant that he was at my mercy for sexual fulfillment. And as the arousal I felt earlier vanished, I focused on doing my job with precision in order to get him off as soon as possible.

Lover Boy didn't have any particular style. It changed all the time depending on his mood. But today, it was rough and hard. Even being in my most loathed position of doggy style, I still felt in control of my emotions. Enjoying the act equated to my fear of losing restraint. It never occurred to me the importance of why I had to feel in control, only that I knew I had to be. In hindsight, it was to prevent myself from being transported back to that six-year-old girl and not being able to govern the outcome of the situation.

When Lover Boy finally climaxed, he tenderly wrapped the blanket around me to keep me warm and whispered in my ear, "You're amazing," as we both succumbed to exhausted satisfaction.

I woke up the next morning to the smell of coffee as I walked into the kitchen to find Lover Boy making breakfast. I couldn't help but smile as I watched him delightfully pull out a batch of homemade granola from the oven while checking on his homemade yogurt.

Could he be any more perfect?

I loved that he was big on healthy eating and the use of organic products. I was beginning to educate myself with the benefits of an organic diet and I found Lover Boy's tree-hugging lifestyle very appealing.

"Mmmm... smells delicious. Is that for me?" I asked, eyeing the glass of orange juice on the table.

"Of course it is. I remembered that you don't drink coffee. It's fresh-squeezed juice just for my Lucy!"

"Why are you so wonderful?" I asked and gave him a warm embrace from behind.

"Why are *you* so wonderful?" he responded. "Come and sit down. I want to talk to you about something."

I sat down at the kitchen table while Lover Boy served me the granola and yogurt with fresh fruit.

"What is it?" I asked curiously.

"Well, I was thinking of going to Thailand in two weeks," he said excitedly.

"That's great! Have you booked your flight yet?" I asked.

"No, I just decided on this when I woke up this morning."

"How long are you planning on going for?"

"Well, I can only take two weeks off work, so I was thinking of going at the end of the month since my business is kind of slow right now."

"Well, who's going to take care of your business if you go?"

"Well, I've got a couple of trusty employees. It's not that difficult. It's a construction supply company. People call in and place their order and we deliver it. My staff will be able to handle it."

"That's so exciting. You're so spontaneous! I wish I could be like that."

"Well, you can because I want you to go with me!"

"You what!?" I asked in shock, trying not to spit up my orange juice.

"Yes, I want you to come with me. I don't want to go alone. I want you with me."

Fuuuccckkk!!! That's when I'm going to be in Bali with Beaver.

"Wow! I don't know what to say. I'm a little shocked."

"Say you'll go with me," he pleaded.

"But it's going to be a very expensive trip for you if I come."

"Well, I'm sure we can work something out."

"I don't know yet. Can I think about it? Because the timing is really close to when university starts and I can't miss any classes," I fabricated.

"Okay. Think about it and let me know in a few days because I need to start booking things."

"Okay, I will," I answered as I mulled over how I could cancel my vacation with Beaver.

༄

CHAPTER 25

BEAVER'S CONTRACT UP NORTH HAD expired a few months back and he was now living with me. I should have been ecstatic that my boyfriend was back, but I found it to be rather annoying because he was now demanding more of my precious time that I couldn't afford to give him. I really couldn't understand how he managed not to show any jealousy or resentment towards me going out night after night with clients. Instead he was patient and understanding to the fact that I was putting him on the back burner. I didn't even stop to think how he was able to endure a one-sided relationship that solely benefited me and wasn't fulfilling any of his physical or emotional needs. I was acting as I always have been... completely selfish.

Much to my dismay, Beaver uncharacteristically poured his heart out to me when I actually paused one afternoon from my hectic schedule to unselfishly ask him, "Are you okay?"

I felt a pang of guilt for not having the awareness that Beaver was in a slump. Beaver was facing insecurities such as how inadequate he was feeling for not being the one to make more money in the relationship. At the same time, he was experiencing horrendous reoccurring nightmares about ripping out his teeth which was the first time that we had ever discussed his teeth which was a sensitive topic.

Always the problem solver, I asked Beaver, "Would you feel better if you fixed your teeth?"

"Of course," Beaver replied. "But I looked into it and I can't afford it."

"What if I helped you?" I offered.

"You don't have to," Beaver dismissed.

"But I want to. Let me help you," I insisted, knowing that I owed him that much for helping me get through the whole pot ordeal.

"Okay. I'll accept your help but there's something else that I really want from you."

"What is it?" I questioned.

"Remember when we first met and we kept planning on going to Bali together but then it never happened...?"

"Yes...," I replied, motioning him to continue.

"Well, I would really like for us to go to Bali. I mean we can afford it now and I've got some time before I have to go back to work. We never spend any time together because of how busy you are. Look... you need a vacation and so do I," Beaver continued as he tried to persuade me. "I just want to connect with you again. I don't think you understand how hard it is for me to have to deal with your job but I try, so now I'm asking you to try for us."

Even though I didn't want to break the good momentum I was experiencing with work, it was heartbreaking to see Beaver plead his case and for once I decided to put Beaver's needs above my own and agree on the trip.

"Okay, we can go to Bali but with one condition," I demanded.

"What is it?" Beaver asked.

"That I pay for the trip because my job is hard on you and I want to thank you for being there for me and for sticking by me."

I was trying to buy my way out of the guilt I felt towards my absence in the relationship just as a parent does when they spoil their kids with material possessions to compensate for their lack of time.

"Okay...," Beaver hesitated.

As much as I wanted to go to Thailand with Lover Boy, I didn't know how I could convince Beaver to postpone or cancel our trip – especially when he had taken it upon himself to plan out all the details to ensure that it was extra special and romantic. But the money was too good to give up and I was already spewing with resentment over the thought that Beaver would not give me my way, so I was going to have to somehow sweet-talk Beaver into agreeing.

"We need to talk," I blurted out as soon as Beaver came home.

"Is everything okay?" he asked, concerned.

"Everything is fine. It's just that I got another work opportunity. One of my clients wants me to go with him to Thailand for two weeks."

"Well, that's good," Beaver said, trying to force a smile across his face.

"I know. The money will be really good. The only thing is he wants to go at the end of the month which overlaps with our holidays."

"Well then, tell him you can't go. Tell him you're already going away on holidays at that time with your boyfriend," Beaver remarked in a snide tone.

"Well, that's what I wanted to talk to you about. I really want to take this job. Can we postpone our trip or are you okay spending a week by yourself in Bali and I can fly from Thailand to meet you there?"

Please, please, please be okay with that!

"No fuckin' way!" Beaver exploded. "This is supposed to be our time to-gether and now you're telling me that I have to spend a week there by myself. It's always all about money with you. You're already making a ton of money but you keep wanting more. What's more important to you… making money or our relationship?"

Making money.

"Of course our relationship," I lied. "But this is a good opportunity. No girls ever get booked for trips!"

"Yeah, well, you're already going to London, so maybe this guy can line up like the rest of us just to take you on vacation," Beaver said.

I knew Beaver was livid because he had the tendency to talk sarcastically when he was really upset. Always a calm guy, this was one of the rare times in our three years together that I'd seen him this worked up. I could have broken up with him to take the job and give myself the complete freedom to do as I wish without any remorse. I would have, had I not cared more about Beaver than I did myself. But, in all honesty, as much hindrance as I felt the relation-ship occasionally weighed on my job, I still liked coming home to the comforts of someone I trusted. Beaver was one of those rare people who possessed that. No matter how much of my time was spent occupied with other men, I still felt a void inside of me that I couldn't quite understand. Beaver was the one to temporarily give me solace because of the security he offered knowing that he was part of my bizarre journey.

"You know what? You're right. I won't take the job. We'll just stick to the original plan," I replied bitterly.

CHAPTER 26

ɋb

IT'S AMAZING WHAT THREE SLEEPING pills could do. I was knocked out cold and only awoke when the flight attendant tapped on my shoulders to inform me that we'd be landing in Heathrow in thirty minutes. I went to the bathroom to freshen up and the mirror reflected a pale face with dark bags. Concealer, blush, and lipstick can be a lifesaver at times. By the time the plane landed, I was looking somewhat human again.

I was beyond thrilled to be in London but at the same time nervous about how the week would pan out with Rock Boy. I was completely taken aback, because of Rock Boy's paranoid nature, when a few weeks ago he asked me to meet him for lunch to give me my first half's payment. I knew it was a huge risk he was taking to be seen in public with me but when he told me the name of the restaurant, I realized that it was a calculated risk. The restaurant was known for its privacy. Perhaps it was his way of testing if we were compatible in the real world as opposed to always being in a hotel room. If that were the case, then I'd say our first-ever interaction in public went seemingly well.

"How was your flight?" Rock Boy asked as we made our way through the crowd.

"It was great. I slept most of the way," I replied politely while trying to hide my disdain for his attire.

God, does he ever wear anything other than jeans and that ugly navy sweater?

"We can either take the fifteen-minute bullet train to the city center but then you won't be able to see any scenery… or we can take the longer train and you'll be able to see more. Which one do you prefer?" he asked as he carried my luggage for me.

"It doesn't matter. You decide," I lied.

The fast train. I just want to get there ASAP.

"Okay then, let's take the longer train. It's about an hour but you'll be able to see the London suburbs."

"Okay, sounds great," I lied again.

It was the longest hour of my life. I was feeling terribly jet-lagged and the wet, cold air was seeping into my bones making me uncomfortable. The grey, dreary skies did nothing to elevate my mood as I tried hopelessly to divert my attention to the scenery outside which was nothing but cramped streets lined with rows of mature brick townhomes. It wasn't until we pulled into the city that I was stunned by the magnificent iconic landmarks surrounded by old European architecture.

I was not disappointed when we stepped out of London's famous black taxi to our luxurious hotel. I even had to take a couple of minutes to admire the plush suite that Rock Boy had reserved for us. The suite was decorated in traditional elegance and had everything one would expect in a five-star hotel.

Wow! He must have paid a fortune for this room!

"I had to book two rooms," Rock Boy informed me.

"Why? Are we staying in separate rooms?"

Please say yes. That would be so awesome.

"No, we're staying in the same room."

Damn it!

"I needed to reserve two rooms in case my wife calls and asks for me and the front desk accidentally tells her I'm here with someone."

How paranoid can he be? Like that's going to happen! What a waste of money.

"So I have one room under my name and one under yours. Do not answer the phone if it rings," he instructed in a serious and authoritative tone.

Take it easy, asshole.

"Sure, no problem. I won't answer it."

"Okay. Well, did you want to go for dinner soon?" he asked, easing up his tone.

"Yes, that would be great," I replied, trying to sound chirpy. "Do you mind if I have a shower first?"

"Sure. We can leave in an hour."

"Sounds good," I replied, faking a smile.

We had an enjoyable evening indulging in fine Italian food over light conversation followed by a leisurely stroll around central London. Keen on being a good tour guide, Rock Boy gave me a little bit of a history lesson as we walked past Buckingham Palace onto the Palace of Westminster that bolstered the Clock Tower—Big Ben—in all its famous glory.

I was fascinated by the antiquity of it all and clung onto all of Rock Boy's words. When we walked across the London Bridge over the famed Thames River, I stood on the bridge to absorb the sight of the London Eye. I had to pinch myself because I couldn't believe that I was in London. Somehow amidst the chaos of my imperfect life, I stood still long enough to marvel in the beauty of such an amazing city. I never thought that my impoverished upbringing would allow me to travel to Europe, a place I always dreamed of visiting but uncertain of how I could manifest it. Never in a million years could I have imagined that it would be under the pretense of a hired call girl accompanying a wealthy client.

I was lucky enough to get a free pass to go sightseeing by myself one day because Rock Boy had a meeting he had to attend.

"You should visit Piccadilly Circus. It's like the Times Square of New York," Rock Boy suggested. "I think you'll like it."

New York was also on my bucket list of places I wanted to visit. Times Square was something I'd only experienced through a television but it always seemed so alluring with all its electrifying billboards and lights. If Piccadilly Circus resembled that, then I most certainly was looking forward to it and it was refreshing to know that I would have some time on my own.

It's true what they say, 'If you really want to know someone, then all you have to do is travel with them,' because his habits were annoying me tremendously. He was a terrible 'aimer.' What I mean by that is his urine never seemed to find its way into the toilet but rather splattered on the floor. If that wasn't disgusting enough, I hadn't seen him change clothes the entire time or maybe he just had ten pairs of the same outfit that he rotated. As well, he also ate off my plate whenever we had a meal, which is a major pet peeve. Nonetheless, this all made me appreciate Beaver more and I found myself missing him.

"And about tonight," Rock Boy continued, "I thought you might like to catch a play."

The word 'play' caught my attention immediately as I've always fancied live theater.

"I'd love that! What show were you thinking of?" I exclaimed.

"I don't know. You pick."

"Phantom of the Opera!" I screeched, having no idea what the musical was about but it was the first thing that came to mind.

"Okay, I'll arrange for the tickets. Make sure you stick around Piccadilly Circus. It's a touristy area with plenty of shops and restaurants, so you'll be safe there," Rock Boy instructed.

He wasn't all that bad in an authoritative kind of way because he did seem to care about my well-being. Both our controlling personalities was what made me clash with him because I was used to getting my way but with him, I had to remind myself daily that I was getting paid to play the part of a submissive. But getting paid extraordinarily well didn't make the intimacy part any easier. His domineering ways were always amplified in the sexual fantasies that he made me play out for him involving anything from role-playing to dressing up in provocative lingerie.

With Rock Boy there was only one way that he liked it and that was aggressive. Having him ram his genitals so hard inside of me was often painful and my only consolation was the big stack of hundreds that was tucked away in my luggage. The ferocity to which he sexed was equivalent to that of a person half his age which made me suspect that he was a sexually repressed person or possibly a sex addict.

My one fuck per booking rule obviously didn't pertain to this booking, so numerous mornings and evenings were filled with sex romps that involved me highly faking my way through it. I agonized every second of it. To endure, I would imagine that I was on a beach drinking fresh coconut water to help me escape the desolate feeling of a worthless human being and the intense anger I felt towards myself for letting him use my body for his own gratification. It was the only time since I started escorting that I questioned if the money was worth it.

Piccadilly Circus turned out to be an interesting afternoon of people watching and much-needed time to myself. Phantom of the Opera turned out to be a huge disappointment because it failed to capture my attention or maybe I was just exhausted from the week. However, the silence between Rock Boy and me during the production was so welcoming that I embraced the moment.

That evening while lying in bed half asleep, Rock Boy tenderly whispered in my ears, "I have a surprise for you."

"What is it?"

"Well, I thought that tomorrow being our last night here we can get dressed up and go have dinner on the Thames River. There's a boat that cruises down the river that serves dinner with dancing afterwards. How would you like that?"

"That sounds lovely," I murmured. Rock Boy surprised me with another sweet gesture by affectionately holding me in his arms while I drifted into a light sleep, unsure if I was dreaming or if he did indeed have a soft side to him.

Dinner on the Thames River while watching the sunset turned out to be lovely and, to my delight, it was the first time that Rock Boy wore something other than his usual uniform. Reflecting on my week, even though at times it was difficult and I had to bite my tongue in order not to scream my true feelings, I still relished in the experience of being able to enjoy a luxurious vacation in a very expensive locale. I put aside my mixed feelings and did my best to enjoy my last night in London. The three-course meal was delicious and I managed to laugh my way through the evening in full acknowledgement that it was the best night I had with Rock Boy.

CHAPTER 27

ᘯ

TRUE TO HIS WORDS, THE first night in Bali, Beaver arranged for a romantic candlelight dinner on the beach. As I followed Beaver along the pathway that led to the beach, I took a deep breath and inhaled the freshness of the ocean air and as I exhaled, I tried to release all the animosity that I felt towards Beaver, for not being flexible with our trip so that I could accompany Lover Boy to Thailand, in order to enjoy our holidays.

"Oh my God! You arranged this just for us?" I asked. I glanced around to observe a table set for two, encapsulated by lit candles and the illumination of the moon, with the sounds of the waves adding to the ambience.

"Yes, it's just for the two of us. I told you that I wanted this trip to be as romantic as possible," Beaver beamed.

"Well, thank you. This is the first time I've ever dined on the beach," I marveled.

"Isn't it great? Finally, I get you all to myself for two weeks. No more of you running off to work every night."

"Yes. It'll be wonderful," I replied as I tried to keep my mind focused in the moment.

That evening was supposed to be the start of an idyllic vacation but after a week of nothing but lazing around, even though my body was as relaxed as could be, my mind was brewing hostile thoughts. Even the paradise of Bali with its crystal clear skies and perfect weather couldn't contain the scrutiny of my own cancerous judgments on myself. I hated having down time because that meant that instead of resting, I would analyze my life which always resulted in me tormenting myself for not accomplishing enough.

I prefer to run at full speed, basking in the joy of being ridiculously busy and over-worked. Being busy left me no time to feel. In the solitude of my own numbness, I would focus on getting from point A to B and when halfway to point B I'd already be thinking of how to get to point C. I was never the type to stop and smell the flowers because to me it was always about the destination and not the journey.

Here I was, a victim of my own atrocious cycle: once I arrive at the destination, it's never as I imagined. The initial goal of escorting to pay off my debts has long absolved and now I was very financially comfortable. But, I was still restless. The happiness that I envisioned was greeted by a deep void of not being good enough.

I spent many idle afternoons lying on the white beaches of Bali trying to conceptualize a new image of jubilation and how I could achieve it. That resurrected a conversation I had with Carmen some years ago of what I would do with my life if I had nothing standing in my way. Carmen was on hiatus from her contract working on a cruise line and we decided to catch up over dinner.

"How's work going?" I asked.

"Life on the ship is good for me because the culture is very accepting of gay couples. So, I get to work with my girlfriend and nobody is judging us," Carmen explained.

"Well, I bet you're glad to be out of the house as well. Now you don't have to deal with Mom and Dad," I said envying Carmen's freedom.

"Yeah, that too," she replied smiling. "How's work for you? Do you like massaging?"

"It's all right but I don't want to do it forever. I'd like to open up some kind of business eventually."

"If you can open up any business right now and money wasn't an issue, what would you open?" Carmen asked curiously.

I paused to think it over before I blurted out, "A spa. I would open up the biggest, most beautiful spa in the city."

After my first spa experience at nineteen years old, I became addicted to the feeling of tranquility that came alongside going to a spa. Being in a spa and enjoying the nourishing elements of a massage and steam melted away all the anger that I felt inside long enough that it left me longing for more. I couldn't think of a better idea than to own my very own spa so that I could have an endless supply of serenity. Of course when I dream it's often big, so the spa would ooze luxury and indulgence, but that came with a hefty price tag that even my newfound money couldn't yet afford.

I spent the remainder of my time in Bali questioning why I was still with Beaver. The vacation was meant to reconnect us and have us enjoy each other's company. Instead, I found Beaver's presence absolutely boring and having sex with him seemed so forceful. I knew the relationship had run its course and I couldn't guilt my conscious into staying with Beaver any longer. It was a matter of breaking up with him in Bali or when we got back home. The latter option seemed to be the better option because I didn't want to ruin the picturesque image of a happy couple that Beaver believed we were. I gave him the romantic vacation he yearned for. We took long walks along the beach, frolicked in the warm aqua water and found ourselves parasailing high in the sky. Evenings were spent conversing over long dinners as Beaver would always affectionately gaze deep in my eyes and express his utmost love for me.

I had to brace myself for the inevitable when we returned home. I was going to shatter Beaver's heart.

CHAPTER 28

ↄ৮

"HEY YOU. HOW'S IT GOING?" I asked in my most cheerful voice. "How come you haven't called in so long?"

"Oh, I've just been busy with work," Lover Boy responded flatly.

"I don't buy it. What's going on? You've been acting strange since you got back from Thailand."

There was a long pause on the phone before Lover Boy responded, "Well, there is something actually... I wasn't sure whether to bring it up or not."

"Well, what is it?" I asked in full alert.

"You know what? Come by tonight at 8:00. We can talk more then, and I would like to see you."

"Okay, 8:00 it is."

Later on that evening as I made my way to Lover Boy's place, I had a bad feeling in the bottom of my stomach that something was seriously wrong. My intuition was confirmed when Lover Boy revealed, "A week after I came back from Thailand I was at my mechanic's getting my car serviced when I saw a beautiful Asian girl there. Apparently her car had broken down right by the auto shop, so she walked over to get some assistance."

"Okay... and what happened?" I asked apprehensively.

"Well, I asked her out, and on our date she kept talking about this best friend of hers that I swear sounds like it could be you."

"Wait a minute," I interrupted. "What is her name?"

"Tanya."

What the fuck!!!!????

"Okay, go on," I urged, trying to remain as calm as possible.

"She said she had this best friend named Lina who was in Bali with her boyfriend. She described this Lina girl and I swear she sounded so similar to you. I even asked her what car this Lina girl drives and she gave me the exact make, model and color as yours. This is all really strange to me. I can't help but think that you set this whole thing up. Are you spying on me or is this all a sick joke?"

I sat there in utter shock trying my best to hide my emotions and absorb the bomb that had been dropped on my head. What are the chances that the world could be so small that Tanya and Lover Boy would meet and go on a date?

"Did she come over to your place after the date?" I asked in the calmest voice I can muster.

"Yes she did, but what does that have to do with anything?"

"I'm just curious, that's all," I replied after I gathered up my thoughts. "Listen, I don't know who this Tanya girl and her best friend are. This all sounds so strange to me too. Okay, so me and this Lina girl drive the same kind of car and somewhat resemble each other. Maybe it's a huge coincidence. This whole story seems so bizarre for it to even connect. I've been seeing you for months now. You know my story and who I am. I don't have a boyfriend. If I really did have a boyfriend, do you think he would be okay with what I'm doing? Would you be okay with your girlfriend being an escort? What is bothering you so much about this?"

"What's bothering me is if what Tanya's saying is true, then you've lied to me this entire time. I don't even know who you are," Lover Boy expressed.

"Listen... you know who I am. All those moments we had together were real," I spoke truthfully. "So how many dates did you two go on? I know I have no right to ask because that's your own personal business, but this has got you all upset, so I just want to know if you're still seeing Tanya and if we should stop our arrangement."

"No. We went on two dates but it never worked out."

"Well, I really don't know what to say. I don't know who this Tanya girl is. I'm not this Lina person. What do you want me to do? I'm sorry this whole situation has gotten you all confused. God, I'm confused from this too!" I said convincingly.

"I know. I'm sorry. This is why I didn't really want to bring it up with you because none of this makes sense. Look, let's just forget about this entirely, okay?"

"Sure. As long as you're not upset about it anymore."

"Look, I'm fine. I'm glad we cleared the air... and you're right. If you were all mine, I wouldn't want you to escort. I'd make sure I had you all to myself," he said as he pulled me close to him exhibiting a glimpse of his former self.

The entirety of the evening was spent with me suppressing the urge to run home and rip Tanya's head off. I was fuming inside because Tanya had been staying with me since I got back from Bali and not once did she mention Lover Boy. I needed to make sense of the betrayal that I was feeling.

"We need to talk. Is there something you want to tell me?" I asked angrily as I stormed into my house the following morning.

"No... What's wrong?" Tanya asked with an intimated look on her face.

"Are you fuckin' sure? Because I just spent the night with Lover Boy and he told me everything!" I screamed.

Tanya looked down on the floor and paused before confessing, "I'm so sorry. I swear I didn't mean to hurt you."

"What the fuck happened? I need answers!" I shouted.

"Well, when you were in Asia my car broke down, so I walked to the nearby auto shop to get help and there was a guy there waiting for his car to get serviced. We started talking and the next thing you know he asks me out, so I agree. We went on a date and you know me, I hate talking about myself, so naturally I was telling him about my best friend."

"What did you say about me?!"

"Well, I was just basically describing your personality to him and telling him how beautiful you are. I told him you were in Bali with Beaver and then he started asking me very specific things about you. I swear it didn't even dawn on me that this was your client. If I knew, I would have never gone on a date with him," she answered with a look of guilt.

"Okay... so it never dawned on you during dinner but then you went to his fuckin' apartment after! Didn't you clue in when he pulled up to his place that it was Lover Boy! For fuck's sake, you dropped me off twice there when I had to see him! You knew every detail about him down to the car he drove, what he does for work and what he looks like."

"Yes, I know. But I wasn't really thinking. It didn't hit me until I left that night that it was Lover Boy. I'm so sorry. I wanted to tell you many times but I was so scared. I didn't know how."

"Why did you go out with him again after you finally clued in that it was Lover Boy?"

"I only went out with him again because he kept calling me over and over again. I agreed to meet up with him only to tell him straight to his face that I wasn't interested."

"How stupid do you think I am? Do you really expect me to believe this shit? Did you sleep with him too?"

"No, I didn't. I swear. We just made out."

"Well, because I was going to say you should have fucked him and charged him for it!" I screamed, unleashing my pent-up fury. "Were you ever going to tell me about this?"

"Yes, I've been trying to tell you this since you got back but I just didn't know how. I was going to tell you eventually. I'm so scared you're going to end our friendship over this. Our friendship means everything to me and I don't want to lose it," Tanya responded in tears.

"Well then, maybe you should have thought twice before you decided to expose my real identity to my best client! I don't buy your story for a second. Okay, maybe it was a huge coincidence that you stumbled across him and went out on a date with him. I might even buy that part where you're just innocently telling him stuff about me. But c'mon, seriously, when he pulled up to his apartment building, you couldn't put two and two together?"

"I'm stupid, okay? I admit it… I fucked up!"

"I think you're just jealous and want to jeopardize my business. You wanted to be an escort a few months ago and I talked you out of it. Is this your way of getting back at me? Because if it is, I'd say you've accomplished your job!"

"I don't want to be an escort and I'm not trying to jeopardize anything. I made a mistake. I realize that now. I should have told you sooner."

"Listen, it doesn't matter what you say. I don't believe you. The trust is broken. I think you should pack up your things and go!" I shouted as I went to my room and slammed the door.

Tanya's actions split open old wounds and fed into my beliefs that I couldn't trust anyone, especially those closest to me. Tanya was one of the rare people that I felt with certainty would never betray me and before all this, I thought our friendship was invincible because there was nothing I wouldn't do for her and vice versa. All this turmoil left me crying over the state of our friendship and the possibility that her deception has fractured us beyond repair.

My following encounter with Lover Boy was a bit awkward on my behalf. The events that unfolded between Tanya and Lover Boy intertwined too closely between my two worlds, leaving me slightly shell-shocked. However, Lover Boy was back to his old doting ways, almost being extra sweet, like the boyfriend who has upset his girlfriend and was now making it up to her. But I had my guard up with him, unsure if he and Tanya were still seeing each other.

Stop it! That doesn't even make any sense. If he's fucking Tanya, then why would he pay to fuck me?!

"Lucy, I've been doing a lot of thinking and I want to ask you something. Would you say that we really enjoy each other's company every time we're together?"

"Yes, I would say so."

Where's he going with all this?

"Well, I've been seeing you for a while now and to be honest I've dated other girls here and there but they don't make me feel the way you make me feel. I haven't been serious with anybody because every time I'm with another girl, I'm thinking about you. I love being with you."

"Aw, thanks. I love being with you too," I replied.

"You make me so happy every time we're together. You have the most beautiful smile. I love it when you laugh." He paused and reached for my hands. "I guess... what I'm trying to say is... I don't want this to be a business arrangement anymore. I want us to be together. I want to wake up next to you every morning and I really want us to give it a shot."

This is like déjà vu all over again with Coin Boy!

I sat there completely surprised, especially in light of what had just happened.

He must have read the reaction on my face. "You don't have to give me an answer right away," he said. "You can give it some thought. In fact, you should give it some thought. I know this will change things."

He was correct in that being with him would completely alter my existing real life. He would have to know the truth that I was in fact Lina, and that Tanya was my best friend who he indeed went on two dates with and kissed.

"Say something, Lucy. I've never seen you so quiet," Lover Boy urged.

What the fuck!? Is this really happening?

"I'm just a little shocked, that's all. I wasn't expecting this," I replied. "You're right. I will need some time to think about this. How would this all work?"

I asked him the same questions I asked Coin Boy. Would he expect me to quit my job? How would I pay my bills?

"Well, yes. I don't want to share you with anyone," he replied softly. "I want you all to myself. I will support you. You don't have to work anymore. You can just focus on finishing up your degree. I will take care of everything for you while you're in school. We'll take it a step at a time and figure it out as we go, but all I'm saying is you don't have to worry about money."

"That's very generous of you but I'm not used to asking people for money. It would feel very weird to me to ask you for money."

"Well, you don't have to. I'll just deposit money in your account every month and you can do as you please with it. On top of that, I'll still pay for all your bills and rent or if you'd like you can move in with me… I mean not straightaway… when you're ready," he said with sincerity.

I can't believe this. I can't think straight!

"Well, I need some time to think this through. We'll talk about it when I'm ready, but for tonight let's just enjoy each other's company, okay?"

"Okay," he replied with a smile.

He stood up and scooped me up from the couch and carried me to his bed. I giggled for him to put me down but it was too late. He pinned himself on top of me and proceeded to kiss me all over my neck until I was able to relax and succumbed to the wonderful feeling. I don't want to say he made passionate love to me that night because the 'L' word makes me nauseous, but our bodies definitely connected as we rocked in unison for hours.

My mind wrestled for days thinking about Lover Boy's proposal and how much I'd have to accommodate just to be with him. With Coin Boy it was easy to have a fake relationship because I didn't have to make any adjustments. With Lover Boy, he was demanding that I quit my job. There was an urgency to speak to Tanya or Carmen... anyone who could give me some advice, but with me still not responding to Tanya's calls and Carmen back on the cruise, I had no one to turn to.

I came to the full realization that being with Lover Boy would foreshadow the end of Tanya's and my friendship and I wasn't ready to give that up. Although my feelings for Lover Boy were strong, my friendship with Tanya meant more to me than the brief feelings of lust I felt towards Lover Boy. Even though our solidarity was temporarily broken, I felt that it was something I could make amends with—Tanya was irreplaceable, unlike the men that came and went in my life.

The last time that I knew I would see Lover Boy, I made sure to dress extra sexy so that I could leave a lasting impression on him. I put on a form-fitting black dress and silk lingerie underneath just in case I decided to throw one on the house as a thank you for all the business he had given. He must have been feeling the same because he answered the door dressed in a dark blue pin-striped suit.

I don't remember him looking this good.

"Wow! You look hot, Lucy!" he said excitedly. "Come in and let me have a look," he said as he spun me around.

"Thanks. You look great too. Did you just get home?"

"Yeah, I've been in meetings all day... such a pain in the ass. I'm glad it's all over now and I get to see you."

He squeezed me tight and I let my body sink into his arms. Was I more attached to him than I thought I was? Everything felt so nice in that moment that when he let go I reined him in again.

"Are you okay?" he asked tenderly.

"Yeah, I'm fine. I just like it when you hold me."

"Okay, well I can keep holding you."

His cologne was intoxicating and I started second-guessing my decision. After what seemed like a long time I mustered up the courage to say, "I think we need to talk."

"Yes, I've been waiting for you to get back to me about your decision."

We walked over to his couch and sat down. He grabbed my feet and started massaging them as I closed my eyes.

Am I making a big mistake? He's attractive, successful, and adores me. I obviously like him more than I'd like to admit. Maybe I can make this work with him. But how?

"So what have you decided?" he asked patiently.

"Well, I'm really torn because a part of me wants to take your offer. I do care for you –actually a lot more than I'd like to admit. But the more logical side of me tells me that this is never going to work between us."

"Of course it will work if we want it to," he said optimistically. He stopped rubbing my feet and began stroking my hair knowing full well how much I like it.

"It's too complicated. If we didn't meet under the circumstances that we did, then things would be different and I'm certain we would be together and it would be great," I said raising my voice ever so slightly.

He must have sensed the stressful tone because he immediately tried to calm me down. "Shhh... it's okay, Lucy. All I know is that I want to be with you. I don't care about anything else. We'll figure it out together. We are obviously very compatible together and I also care about you very much."

"I've really thought about it and I can't see how this is going to work out in the long run. We can keep our existing agreement and I can come and see you whenever you like but I can't accept your proposal. I'm sorry," I replied choking back tears.

"I don't want to be a client!" he said, raising his voice. "I want you to be mine. All mine. I can't keep seeing you the way we've been seeing each other."

Shit. This is a first. He's never raised his voice, ever.

"Listen to me, Lucy. Don't do this. For crying out loud, give it a chance!"

"I can't, okay? I really can't. I'm sorry. I think I should go," I said.

"Lucy, you do realize that I probably won't call you anymore after this, right?"

I nodded, still holding back my tears.

"I can't keep seeing you because every time I see you I get more and more attached to you and it kills me knowing that I'll never really have you."

"I understand," I nodded as I leaned over and whispered, "Goodbye."

I dashed straight to the door, not bothering to turn around one last time to see him.

It's not supposed to be like this. You were never supposed to get attached.

℘

CHAPTER 29

MY SEVERED BUSINESS TIES WITH Lover Boy oddly enough felt more like a breakup and that started a series of other so-called 'breakups' in my life. Since buying me that cell phone, Coin Boy was calling me at least a couple times a day to whine about how much he missed me but now the calls have dwindled to a few a week. I should have speculated that something was wrong. But my mind was occupied with the whole Lover Boy and Tanya ordeal to notice any changes in mine and Coin Boy's supposed relationship. So it was jarring when Coin Boy broke down and confessed that he'd been cheating on me.

"What do you mean you've been cheating on me? With who?!" I asked more out of curiosity than anything.

"It's a girl from China. We've been talking online the past month and now she wants me to come and visit her," Coin Boy revealed.

"I can't believe this! How can you do this to me?" I asked, continuing my act of a distressed girlfriend.

"I know, I know. I'm so sorry, Laina. It's just that I need more from you and it seems like you keep pushing me away. You don't answer my calls half the time and when you do you're always making up excuses as to why you can't see me. There was that two weeks where you disappeared and I couldn't get hold of you. What was that all about? You keep lying to me," Coin Boy expressed.

Shit, Bali! I knew I shouldn't have left without saying anything.

"I was camping for two weeks. There was no reception. Sorry I didn't tell you," I lied.

"That's what I mean! What kind of girlfriend takes off for two weeks and doesn't tell her boyfriend?"

"What kind of boyfriend cheats on his girlfriend when she's out of town?" I screamed back.

"I thought you dumped me without even explaining why. I was upset and I needed to talk to someone. I'm so sorry, Laina. I didn't mean to hurt you. I love you but I need more from you. This girl... she really cares about me," he shared naïvely.

"Of course she does!" I yelled. "She lives in China and hooking up with a foreigner is her meal ticket to Canada."

"It doesn't seem like that. I know she cares about me because she wants to meet my girls whereas you refuse to see them."

Oh my God! He can't be this dumb. The girl is completely using him!

"I never said that I didn't want to meet your girls. I told you we can discuss it at a later time."

"That's what I mean. You're always pushing things for a later time. You could never commit to anything. I need someone who will fully commit to me!" Coin Boy said.

"Well, what are you going to do? It seems like you've already fallen for her. Are you going to China to see her?"

"Oh, Laina. I've already booked my ticket. I feel so torn. Seeing you here with me... I know I still love you very much but you're not letting me in. This is not the kind of relationship I want. I want you to love me the way that I love you. Everything is so hard with you whereas with her it's so easy."

"Okay, I get it. You want to break up with me so that you can go see this girl in China," I said in an upset tone.

Okay — now cry and act like you're so heartbroken by his decision.

"Oh, Laina. Please forgive me. I never meant to hurt you. I still care about you but I think this is best for the both of us."

I could have left it like that and walked out the door, but instead I opted to pull the biggest guilt trip on Coin Boy in the odd chance that things didn't work out with China girl. I didn't care that he was so-called 'breaking up' with me;

rather, I was upset over the loss of two VIP clients in such a short amount of time and I was brewing over how I could recover the loss of income.

"You know even though you thought I wasn't showing you much affection, I really did care about you. I'm so hurt," I wept.

"I'm so sorry, Laina. I wish you would have shown me this much emotion before. I would have never cheated on you. I feel like the biggest asshole," he said with heartache.

"You should feel like an asshole. You broke my heart," I sniveled, enjoying the mind game I was playing with Coin Boy.

"Well... I guess it's goodbye," I continued as I left him sitting with his face buried in his hands.

Coin Boy truly had a gracious soul. He deserved love that stemmed from a pure place rather than out of a flawed person like me. I was an ugly tormented soul and didn't value myself. Despite all the affection he showed me, I couldn't open my heart to accept that love was real and that I was worthy to receive it. It was safer to hide behind narcissistic tendencies than accept kindness when it came from any man.

CHAPTER 30

꯶

PERHAPS THE HARDEST BREAKUP WAS that of Beaver's because it wasn't under the guise of a false relationship. It was an authentic one that stood by me through challenging times and one that had three years' worth of memories. My superstitious nature convinced me that unwelcomed events always happened in threes, so I had to end my bad luck streak by doing the inevitable.

"Can we talk?" I asked Beaver one evening after dinner.

"Yeah, what is it?" he asked caringly. "Is everything okay?"

"Well, I've been thinking about it a lot lately and I don't really know how to say it so I'm just going to blurt it out. I think we should break up."

"What?! What do you mean you think we should break up? Where did this come from?" he asked in shock.

"I just haven't felt connected in a long time and we're going in different directions."

"Is it something I did?!" he asked, choking back tears.

"No, you didn't do anything. I just don't feel like this relationship is right for me anymore and I don't want to waste any more of your time," I said softly.

"Well, I don't want to break up," he sobbed. "Where did this come from? I thought we were doing fine. We just took a trip together and you took care of me after my dental surgery... I thought things were going well."

"I know... I know," I interrupted. "It's not you. It's me. I simply don't want to be in this relationship anymore. I'm sorry for hurting you. I really didn't mean to," I replied.

"Is it because I don't make enough money... because I'm not as ambitious as you," Beaver said angrily.

True.

"Of course it isn't," I lied.

"Have you met someone else?"

If you only knew...

"No!" I replied, agitated.

"Well, did you ever really love me?"

"Of course I did," I lied again. What was I supposed to say? *"No, you were just conveniently there when I couldn't stand to be alone. You were somewhat of a rebound"*?

"Listen, I know you're upset now but in no time you will be dating and life will be good again. I'm always going to love and care about you as a friend. Can we at least still be friends?" I asked.

"Yes, I still want you in my life in some way," he replied with utmost sadness. "I loved every moment with you."

"So did I."

We sat on the couch wrapped in silence as we held each other tightly. That was exactly how I felt about Beaver because even though we were not going to be romantically involved, I cherished our time together and he had proven himself to be trustworthy and, in doing so, I wanted to maintain a friendship with him regardless.

CHAPTER 31

✄

IT DIDN'T TAKE ME TOO long to adjust to living on my own again once Beaver moved out. And it appeared that once my breakup streak was over, life moved on, and I continued to stay busy with new clients and my existing VIPs. It seemed as soon as I lost Lover Boy and Coin Boy's business, GQ Boy decided to ramp up his bookings and I was seeing him steadily.

One evening, as I was sitting on GQ Boy's lap in his office laughing away at a funny online post, I found our faces inches away from each other and in the spur of that moment, without knowing why, I broke my golden rule of no kissing and locked my lips against his. If any, this kiss should have belonged to Lover Boy but instead it was GQ Boy's lips that were on the receiving end.

My actions left me speechless and GQ Boy in shock as he exclaimed, "You kissed me! Why did you kiss me? I thought that no kissing was one of your rules!"

To this day, I have no answer as to why I kissed GQ Boy. But my theory lies in that maybe we don't have as much control over our lives as we imagine. Possibly, it was to restore my faith that there was a God or higher power that was aligning chains of events so that I could exist in the space I am today. Without that first kiss, I would have had a completely different outcome, but that kiss took me down a path that perhaps was preordained. There are no co-incidences in life and I believe everything does happen for a reason, but it took me a long time to understand the ramifications of that kiss.

Almost immediately after that kiss, GQ Boy exhibited a much needier side that I found rather odd because GQ Boy always displayed great composure, never to show or withhold attachment but somehow managed to balance it perfectly because of his position and influence. He possessed an eloquence that fascinated me because of the wide range of topics we could discuss, so overall I found him to be a well-rounded individual.

He was the only client I ever gave my private number to… my reason being was that he was a sane individual who would only call when he wanted my company. This way I could cut corners with my agency. Part of it was greed but the other part could support my argument that the universe was stewing up something big for me. Regardless, what resulted was many nights spent on the phone with GQ Boy. He would call and ask me how my day was. It wasn't my desire to open myself to him, but he had a way of getting me to divulge my thoughts that made me feel like I was still keeping a far proximity from him.

On one of those phone conversations, GQ Boy asked me, "You're such a smart and witty girl, what are your plans for the future? I can't see you being in your profession for long."

It was a question that I hadn't been asked before by any client. I took GQ Boy's gesture as a sign that he saw beyond the surface of my thick-headed act and recognized some potential in me — that I had the capacity to become something great in this life.

"I would like to open up my own spa one day," I answered.

"Okay, a spa. Why a spa?"

"I don't know," I shrugged. "Because that's what I always dreamed of… and not a cheap spa… a huge, luxurious spa with pools, steam rooms, and saunas."

"Well, how much do you think that's going to cost?"

"I don't know. I haven't looked into it, but off the top of my head… maybe a million dollars."

"A million dollars! Wow… that's a lot!" GQ Boy exclaimed.

"I don't know. Maybe less. I'm just guessing. All I know is that I want it to be huge with lots of amenities because that's what I enjoy when I'm at the spa, so that's what I want to build. Plus, with all the money this city has, we really don't have a nice spa."

"That's true, but how do you plan on building this?"

"I don't know yet."

"Well, maybe I can help you with it. Maybe I can invest in it with you," he offered.

What did he just say? He'll invest in a spa with me?

"Are you serious or joking?" I replied perplexed.

"I'm being serious. Well, you would have to put together a business plan and give me numbers as to the cost. But yeah, I'm being serious."

"Why would you offer this to me?" I questioned.

What's the catch?

"Well, besides the fact that I find you absolutely stunning, I think you have a keen business sense."

"Ummm... okay, thanks... I guess that's the nicest thing anyone has ever told me," I replied, trying to digest what GQ Boy had just offered me.

I couldn't understand what GQ Boy's agenda was to offer me such a lucrative deal. Sure... I was seeing him on a regular basis but it was simply business to me. The unfortunate part with escorting is, the lines between business and personal are often murky, so if that kiss was what sent GQ Boy mixed signals, then I was beginning to regret my actions because I couldn't afford for him to fall in love with me and for me to lose yet another VIP client. His offer seemed too good to be true and I was positive that GQ Boy was far too intelligent to fall for someone like me, so I brushed off our conversation as nonsense and forgot about it until one evening I was hit with another lightning bolt.

After a pleasant evening with GQ Boy, as I got into my car to drive away, he poked his head through my window and dropped the three cringe worthy words: I Love You. Hearing those words sent me into panic mode and all I could do was reply, "Thank you," as I sped away.

Holy shit! Did he just tell me he loves me? How is this even possible? You've got to be kidding.

I decided to call Tanya to discuss and dissect the situation with her. After our fight, it took me some time to build my trust back, and even though it wasn't a hundred percent yet and at times I opted to keep Tanya in the dark about things, I needed advice on this one and she was the only one who knew me.

"I think he has something good to offer you. It's been your dream to open up a spa and he's willing to help, so why not? Let him invest in it. Besides, if it gets you to stop escorting, then I'll support that. I don't want you to escort for the rest of your life. Do you want to do it for the rest of your life?" Tanya asked.

"Of course not. Lately I've had no patience with any of my clients. The industry is starting to wear on me. I don't know how much longer I can do this," I replied exhausted.

"Well, wasn't the original goal to do this long enough to get out of debt? Well, you have no more debt and you've saved a lot of money, so maybe it's time to get out now," Tanya suggested.

"I know, but it all seems too good to be true."

"Listen, he seems head over heels for you and if he's willing to take care of you and invest in your dream, then I say stop overthinking it... quit your job and let this guy take care of you."

"But I don't love him. I mean I like him and we get along but I'm not attracted to him. He's much too old for me. I'm attracted to his wealth and power and the possible opportunities that come with dating him," I shared in honesty.

"Yeah. I already know that," Tanya laughed. "Men have been falling at your feet and you just step all over them. Why are you talking about love when you know you've never believed in it? It's always about business with you, so wouldn't this be just another business decision?" Tanya challenged.

Tanya's assessment of me was spot-on and I was so grateful for her advice. Still, if I was to consider GQ Boy's offer and take advantage of his love for me, then there would be some wrinkles to iron out to make the transition possible.

CHAPTER 32

꼭

AFTER OUR TRIP IN LONDON, there was a stretch of time where I didn't hear from Rock Boy, so I presumed that he had sensed my dislike towards him despite how hard I tried to disguise it. I would have felt no loss if he were to have never called me again but when he did call, I accepted the invitation to meet him.

"It's been a while," Rock Boy addressed.

"Yes, I know. How come you haven't called me?" I directed.

"I've been busy with work. My company is trying to acquire another company, so I've been working around the clock. I had a window this afternoon and that's why I called you," he answered as he pulled me close.

"That's good. I was beginning to think that you had forgotten all about me," I said flirtatiously.

"I don't think I can easily forget you like that," he chuckled.

Our time apart did nothing to strengthen my feelings for him because every minute that he was inside of me felt like ten and I was more than elated when it was over with.

"I need to ask you something," he said after we both got dressed. "Would you like to go to Seattle with me next month for a weekend?"

Seattle! I've never been there... but can I do this with him all over again?

"Of course. I'd love to go with you. Which weekend?" I asked.

"I'll confirm the dates with you but it'll be a Thursday to Monday," Rock Boy replied.

"Okay, sounds good. Is it the same arrangement as London?"

"Sure, if that's okay with you."

"Yes, that works."

Well at least I know it's worth my time.

It was a great opportunity to recoup some financial loss since the splits from Lover Boy and Coin Boy. I was more aware of the scope of work this time around. I persuaded myself that it was only for a few days, so it wouldn't be as bad as London.

Sadly, almost immediately upon checking into our hotel in Seattle, the old feelings of how I felt towards him resurfaced. The difference this time was an internal restlessness that I couldn't suppress no matter how hard my efforts were. My body was physically present but my mind was on GQ Boy and his proposition. My heart was no longer into subjecting myself to others' fantasies no matter how well the pay. I knew I had a lot of internalizing to do and I wasn't going to achieve anything being around Rock Boy, so even though I wanted to leave, I stayed to fulfill my contractual obligations with him.

Rock Boy had a fun-filled weekend planned that was reminiscent of our time in London. Our visit atop Seattle's famed Space Needle should have been wonderful but the heavy rain left me feeling cold and miserable. Even dining at an exquisite establishment and dancing away to a live band did nothing to lift my spirits. I continued to feel more lost with myself.

It was imminent that my frame of mind would result in the two of us clashing and it happened on the morning when we were planning on going to the Pike Place Market. He requested that I dance around in my lingerie for him and even though the idea repulsed me, I gritted my teeth and began swaying my hips back and forth.

What an asshole. Let's get this over with.

I climbed on top of him and continued the lap dance until he had me on all fours and was savagely thrusting himself inside of me like something had possessed him.

"Are you almost done?!" I snapped when I couldn't bear it any longer.

"What? You're not enjoying it?" he groaned.

"Well, I told you to take it easy. You're hurting me," I growled.

"Oh, I'm sorry, I didn't hear you."

Sensing my rejection, Rock Boy stopped as I got up to the bathroom to cleanse myself of him. While standing underneath the cascading warmth of the shower a voice inside me said: "You are done." In that exact moment, I knew that I was finished with escorting.

As if reading my mind, Rock Boy voiced, "I think its best if you arrange an early flight home but I'd still like to have breakfast with you if you want to."

What for? Well why not, it'll be the last time I ever see him.

"Sure," I agreed.

The awkward silence was deafening as we sat in the main dining restaurant of the beautiful hotel before Rock Boy broke the dead air with, "You know, I was really hurt by the way you treated me earlier."

What? He was hurt by what I did?!

"Why were you hurt?" I asked, trying to remain calm.

"Well, when you asked me if I was almost done, it made me feel like you didn't even like me and that you were only here because I paid you to be here."

No shit! That's exactly why I'm here! I can't stand you!

Rather than expressing my true feelings, I decided to toy with his mind and leave him a vulnerable impression of myself so that it wouldn't seem like I was the bitch that ruined the trip. I rolled out another Oscar-worthy performance. I gave my inner thigh a hard pinch to spawn fake tears.

"What do you expect? I've been seeing you for months now and I've completely fallen for you. I know you're married and would never leave your wife and that's why I just feel like such a stupid little girl. We fuck here and there and go on trips but I can never really be with you and that breaks my heart. I have to distance myself from you in order to protect myself and I guess that's why I treated you the way I did earlier because I just can't deal with this anymore," I said.

"I'm so shocked right now. I had no idea you felt that way," he said apologetically.

That's NOT how I really feel about you.

"Why didn't you tell me sooner?" Rock Boy continued.

"What's the point? You would never leave your wife and family to be with me. You've told me over and over again that you would never do anything to jeopardize your family. So how was I going to tell you that I was falling in love with you?"

"You're right, but I still wish you would have told me. All this time I thought you were moody. I just didn't understand how sometimes you were so affectionate and other times you were so cold."

"Well, now you know why."

"Yes I do," he said humbly.

I never saw Rock Boy after that day but his reaction to my deception made me realize that he and I were indeed cut from the same cloth. We both walked around with an invisible shield to protect us from getting hurt and underneath our brash exterior lied an insecure person who was longing for love in all the wrong places. It even occurred to me that the way he sexed was his coping mechanism towards his own demons just as money and ambition was my way of dealing with pain.

CHAPTER 33

꽁

GQ Boy was more than thrilled when, after countless times of unsuccessful persuasion to get me to quit my job and accept his proposition, I finally agreed. After the incident when he dropped the 'L' bomb on me, he continued to flood me with affection and compliments that inflated my ego even more. Even though the physical attraction wasn't there on my behalf, that didn't stop me from delighting in all the attention he was showering on me, especially when it came from an older prominent gentleman.

That evening we found ourselves in his new lavish condo as we celebrated the occasion with lots of laughter and take-out food.

"You've made me a happy man," he beamed relishing in the good news. "I've waited months for this."

"I know. You broke me down," I joked.

"So what changed your mind? Last week you were still adamant that you didn't want to quit because you were too independent to rely on anyone?"

"Let's just say that I've been seriously thinking about your offer to invest in my spa and I'm ready to move forward and start that chapter of my life," I responded truthfully.

"That's great! And what about us?" GQ Boy inquired.

"What do you mean?"

"Does this mean we're together? You're all mine?"

Why do all men have such as sense of ownership?

"Of course," I replied, knowing full well what the terms of his investment entailed.

Besides having a business relationship, it would also imply having a personal one. Some may see it as a form of continued prostitution but in the end are we all not prostituting ourselves out in one way or another? Our time on Earth is so finite that when we engage in activities that we loathe we become prostitutes to life itself. The unfortunate part is most of our time is occupied in things we dislike rather than embellishing the things that bring us joy.

My relationship with GQ Boy is one I see as opportunistic. He offered me financial security and a jet-setting lifestyle on a silver platter, all the things that I was brainwashed from childhood to believe that mattered. Given the latter choice of prolonged escorting or a life basked in luxury with the potential of owning a successful day spa, the choice was obvious to me, especially coming from my broken views on love.

The transition period between taking our relationship from escort and client to the real world happened effortlessly because he accepted all of who I was—the pot growing, the escorting—without casting judgment but instead with empathy for all my growing pains, and for that I respected him. There wasn't too much to explain to our families because my family always viewed me as a wild child who did as I pleased. He wasn't close enough to his own to even give an explanation. GQ Boy didn't have friends *per se* but more business acquaintances that under an unwritten code never asked the details of how we met. With me there was Tanya who already knew everything.

Our courtship took us all over the world to places I only dreamed of visiting. On one occasion while we were riding camels along the backdrop of the great pyramid of Giza, I recognized that there was nothing this man wouldn't do to make me happy. Just that knowledge made me feel so secure. In a twisted way, he represented the ideal father figure that I longed for as a child.

On another trip atop the Eiffel Tower, when he kissed me and said, "I love you more and more each day," it filled me with great warmth knowing that I was loved by someone. In turn, my heart opened up the best it knew how, into a caring manner. Our relationship wasn't one of lust on my part but rather companionship. Luckily for me, GQ Boy didn't push me for more. It only further perpetuated his desire to keep me content. He continued to whisk me away on weekend trips to New York to shop along Fifth Avenue or relax on the beach in Hawaii in the comforts of five-star accommodations. Needless to say, I loved the lifestyle he provided. Outwardly it was a happy time in my life but inwardly that dark feeling of self-hatred still lingered, regardless of the amount of material wealth that I was surrounded by.

CHAPTER 34

๛

GQ BOY AND I WERE very compatible in every aspect of our personal relationship. We rarely fought because he always gave me my way. However, when it came to the spa and the vision I had for it, that's when we had our disagreements.

"What do you think?" I asked excitedly after six months of arduous work to complete the business plan for the spa.

"I think it's really good, but don't you think it's too big? I mean, it's going to cost $1.5 million. Originally you said it would be around $1 million. I'm concerned this is going to be too much for you to handle," he answered in a concerned tone.

"No, it'll be fine. I can do it. I won't compromise my vision," I said firmly.

"We'll have to have at least forty people in per day to even break even. That's a lot. And keep in mind you're just estimating the lease costs right now. We haven't even found a space yet, so the lease could be much higher than this which would mean you'd have to have at least fifty people through a day to break even."

"Don't you notice that you act so different towards me every time we talk about business?" I asked upset.

"Well, I'm a numbers guy and these numbers are outrageous!" he replied.

"Well, if you don't want to invest in it, then say so," I shouted. "I've worked my ass off to get this plan ready. I got all the numbers and broke down every single cost for you. The report is fuckin' perfect and now you're saying it's outrageous," I yelled.

"Calm down. All I'm suggesting is we start off with a smaller spa and slowly expand. I'm just trying to be practical because I don't want you to fail. I want you to succeed."

"I'm going to succeed because I'll die before I let the spa fail," I answered immaturely as I got up to leave.

"Fine. Just leave like you always do," GQ Boy bellowed.

What he suggested fell on deaf ears. I was inexperienced with business and instead of taking his advice, my naïveté made me think that the grandeur and opulence of a world-class spa would automatically attract customers. What I should have done was humble myself and take note as he shared the ins and outs of how to operate a successful business. But, my young self thought that I had it all figured out.

Eventually, I did compromise with GQ Boy when I agreed on a moderately smaller space in a promising central location. Afterwards, my plan was to match GQ Boy's initial investment so that we would have an equal partnership. I almost preferred it that way because that represented equal control and power for me. It made me feel like I wasn't using him to open my spa but rather it was a fair business deal. Most of the money I had saved during my escorting days would be placed in the spa, but it was a risk I was willing to take to achieve my goals. It wasn't exactly a calculated risk but more of an ego trip to prove my place and capability in the world.

I was left to my own devices on a creative level to obsess over all the little details of the spa. I even welcomed leaked emails that deemed me a "bloodsucking bitch who was impossible to work with because of how anal [I was]." I didn't like people enough to care for their thoughts nor did I trust people enough to want to befriend them, so I brushed off their comments as nothing more than me protecting my company and ensuring the success of it. In addition, I got caught up in believing that I was better than those who weren't in reach of wealth, so my falsified confidence only got inflated while with GQ Boy.

When the time came to hire an Assistant Spa Director, I couldn't think of anyone better for the job than Carmen. She had just finished ten years working on the cruise ship and was ready to come home for good. So, I took that opportunity to take her out for lunch and offer her the job.

"Do you remember years ago when we went out for dinner and I told you that my dream was to build a luxury spa?" I asked.

"Yes, I remember that," Carmen replied.

"Can you believe its happening?! Sometimes it feels so surreal!"

"I'm so proud of you," Carmen gleamed.

"Thanks," I replied. "Do you judge me for being with GQ Boy? I mean most people see me as this big gold digger who's with him for his money."

"No. I may have disagreed about your career choices at times," Carmen said. "But GQ Boy is a big boy and he knows what he's getting into. I'm keen on anything that doesn't involve you escorting because you know I wasn't supportive of that decision."

"I know," I replied shamefully. "Remember all those times you would take me on all those open casting calls because Mom and Dad refused to?" I asked, changing the topic.

"Yeah, they thought your dreams of becoming an actress were so foolish," Carmen said.

"You were always so encouraging of all my dreams and aspirations."

"Well, that's 'cause you're my sister and I love you."

"You're the best sister," I smiled, so grateful for our close bond. "Well, now that you're back, what are you planning on doing for work?"

"I don't know yet. I was going to take a couple of months off and then start looking for something."

"Well, do you want to work at the spa with me? I need an Assistant Spa Director. I think you'd be perfect for it."

"Okay, let me think about it but you probably know what my answer will be. You've always gotten your way with me."

I like getting my way.

CHAPTER 35

૪

A MONTH BEFORE THE OPENING of the spa, I found myself walking alone through the space as I finally allowed the realization of my dream to seep into consciousness. I'd been so busy over the last three years meticulously seeing through every aspect of the spa from conceptualization to design to construction that I never partook in memorable moments along the way. As I mentioned, in my eyes, the importance lied in the arrival.

It didn't matter that the journey in the last few years involved many sleepless nights when I'd find myself awake over design and construction mishaps. The biggest stress factor was the ballooning costs and somehow managing to rein it in to appease GQ Boy who was breathing down my neck not to go over budget.

Through sweat and tears, I stuck to my vision and the end product was astounding. The city's very first mineral pool, an 8,000 square feet of contemporary opulence, was encapsulated in frosted glass and infused with forty different minerals from the sea. Along with the mineral pool, the spa was equipped with steam rooms and rain showers as well as a co-ed sauna.

The lighting in the spa was kept fairly dim with the highlight being the royal blue LED lights that lined the hallway showcasing the dark customized ten-foot-tall sliding doors. Each of the ten treatment rooms had its own state-of-the-art equipment complete with an electronic massage bed that could move up and down with a push of a button, crisp white sheets that were topped with a satin duvet and, towel and oil warmer.

The relaxation lounge was separated from the hallway with a decorative glass partition and furnished in all-white chaise lounges. On one side of the room was the refreshment area with an assortment of teas, snacks, and flavored water. On the opposite side was a built-in magazine wall that displayed thirty different types of magazines.

The entrance of the spa featured a very grand water feature cascading in front of the huge spa logo. A modern chandelier hung above the sitting area. Off to the side of the sitting area were the luxurious pedicure chairs. They were fit for a queen with built-in massagers, comfortable headrests, oversized arms, and pipeless technology that ensured the highest standard in safety. In sum, there were three pedicure and manicure stations, all sticking with the all-white furniture theme contrasting nicely against the dark floors.

The spa also extended to a large open yoga room in which the entire back wall was a mesh lit screen that illuminated the entire room. Next to the yoga room was the private gym used for personal training that came equipped with the finest equipment.

Dreams really do come true.

My vision had completely sprung to life as I marveled in astonishment what sheer tenacity could achieve. The odds were stacked up against me from day one, but somehow my voyage had taken me from a dreadful childhood to a pot grower to an elite call girl and now the proud owner of a multimillion-dollar spa, all by the age of twenty-eight. I felt on top of the world.

CHAPTER 36

ゆ

ONCE THE FRUITS OF MY labor came to life and I knew that owning my own
spa was imminent, I scrupulously planned out my life with precision. On a
personal level, I was content with GQ Boy and wanted to see our relationship continually blossom. Life with GQ Boy required minimal effort because
we were two people who thrived on success and had careers that demanded
a lot of time, so we understood to give each other space when necessary. At
home, GQ Boy was very laid-back and appreciated that I made all the mun-
dane decisions as to where to vacation or what to eat, which satisfied my
controlling ways. Over the course of three years we built a high level of trust
with one another which resulted in both of us feeling blessed and secure in
the relationship.

When it came to business, I put enormous pressure on myself to ensure
that the spa would be successful with the vision to build additional spas once
the first one took off. GQ Boy was on board with my plan and supported me
wholeheartedly because he just wanted to see me flourish.

However, there was one thing not planned and that was Aiden. Upon meeting him it felt like my world had been struck by a massive lightning bolt that
veered me off my carefully devised course into uncharted territory.

A brief introduction to Aiden during the construction of the spa didn't leave
much of an impression on me, only that his magnetizing blue eyes managed to
captivate me long enough to assess that he was well-spoken for his young age.
After that meeting, I completely forgot about Aiden until he showed up at the
spa towards the end of construction to see the progress. It was towards the end

of a workday and the trades were scurrying to leave, so I took the liberty to give Aiden a tour of the space. This time around I actually took a good look at Aiden and found him to be very attractive.

When we ended the tour in the gym, I couldn't help but ask Aiden, "How old are you?"

"I'm twenty," he replied innocently.

"Oh my God. You're just a baby!" I exclaimed.

"Well, how old are you?" he asked, batting his long lashes.

"I'm twenty-eight," I answered.

"Well, you don't look your age. I thought you were younger."

"Thanks. Do you have a girlfriend?" I stammered, feeling the foreign effects of butterflies.

Why am I so nervous?

"No, I just got out of a relationship. What nationality are you?" he asked with curiosity.

"I'm Vietnamese."

"Oh, I love Vietnamese food!" Aiden declared.

"That's great! Maybe I can make you some Vietnamese food one of these days," I flirted.

What's wrong with me?

"I'd love that," he responded with flushed cheeks.

That's cute. He's blushing.

"So do you own the spa by yourself or are there investors involved?" he asked.

"I own half of it and the other half is owned by my business partner who's more of a silent partner," I replied in half-truth.

Why didn't I tell him that my business partner is also my boyfriend?

"Wow! You're really successful for someone your age," Aiden said.

"No, just hardworking," I answered.

Shit! My hands are sweating!

"Sorry, I've got to go. My parking is about to expire," Aiden said. "I really enjoyed talking to you and thanks for the tour. The spa is beautiful."

"Thanks," I replied, feeling slightly bummed that he had to leave.

"Here's my number in case you ever need to get a hold of me," Aiden said as he passed me his business card.

"Thanks. It was nice talking to you, too." I politely replied, holding back my desire to kiss him.

What the fuck is going on?

CHAPTER 37

❦

I RUSHED HOME AND, BEFORE I even took off my shoes, I was already dialing Tanya's number.

"Something weird is happening to me," I blurted out as soon as Tanya answered.

"What happened? Is everything okay?" Tanya asked in concern.

"I think so. I'm not sure. I met this guy and strange things started happening to me!" I said, panic-stricken.

"What happened!?" Tanya exclaimed.

"Well, I started to get really nervous and... you know... when I get nervous my hands get all clammy. My heart was racing but at the same time I had butterflies in my stomach. I can't even remember the last time I had butterflies!" I yelled.

"Whoa... slow down! Who's the guy? I want every detail," Tanya demanded.

"His name is Aiden and he's the son of the general contractor I hired. I gave him a tour of the spa and we started talking... he's so frickin' hot! In a boyish way and the whole time, I couldn't keep it together."

"What does he look like?"

"He's tall... like six feet... but skinny... He's got this cute wavy brown hair and these amazing eyes!"

"Sounds like you have a crush on him," Tanya said bluntly. "How old is he?"

"That's the thing... he's only twenty," I moaned.

"Shit, he's a kid!" Tanya called out.

"I know. This is not like me. I'm so baffled as to why I'm feeling like this."

"Well, you've always been a sucker for a baby face. Did you tell him you had a boyfriend?"

"No," I replied, feeling guilty. "He never really asked so I didn't say anything. I know he's single."

"Listen, I think it was an 'in-the-moment' thing. You saw someone that you found attractive. When was the last time you found anyone attractive? So you got a little stirred up. By tomorrow you'll forget about the kid and everything will be fine," Tanya advised.

"I hope so," I replied with uncertainty.

My abrupt infatuation with Aiden did not dissipate overnight as I hoped. When I walked into the spa the following day, the sight of Aiden dressed in full-on construction gear turned me on and I found myself wanting him.

What is wrong with you? He's too young.

No matter how much sense I tried to make out of the situation, the chemistry between us was undeniable as we flirted with each other. There was enough electromagnetic energy pulsating between us to light the entire spa. Before we knew it, we found ourselves tucked away in the sauna. As we sat there, Aiden planted his warm lips on mine and I welcomed the kiss like a person deprived of affection. Every touch resonated sensations in my body that I thought were lost years ago when Miguel broke my heart; but this time around, the intensity was amplified tenfold.

The butterflies, the fireworks, time standing still... as cliché as it sounds, that's exactly how I felt in that moment. The overwhelming connection I felt with Aiden was enough for me to ignore my conscious questioning of how one could stir up this much nostalgia in such a short amount of time, and contend to the utter bliss that had me wrapped. We pulled away long enough to gasp for air before our mouths would collide in perfect unison of tongue and lips and our bodies moving in rhythm to our sexual desires.

A call from one of the tradesmen brought us back from euphoria and left me with the full realization that that kiss had just opened up Pandora's Box.

CHAPTER 38

᯼

THAT NIGHT AS I LAY restlessly in bed, my mind was tormented by that kiss. The righteousness in me told me to forget about Aiden and refocus my attention on my only love – the spa. Any unfavorable actions could jeopardize the spa and kissing another guy when your business partner is also your lover would be digging yourself a grave. At the same time, my yearning to replicate the feeling of kissing Aiden only added fuel to my burning desire to sleep with him, if only once, to satisfy my libido. When I could no longer handle the banter of right and wrong, I decided to call Tanya for some much-needed advice.

"What is it?" Tanya asked in a sleepy voice

"I kissed Aiden today..."

"What! Okay, I'm up now. You've got my full attention," Tanya screeched.

"Well, he kissed me first."

"Is he a good kisser?"

"He's a great kisser. Just the right amount of tongue and no slobbering. It was perfect!" I relished.

"Wow, how did this happen? You just met."

"I know. It's so crazy and I'm so confused right now. I'm feeling all these emotions that I don't even know how to describe and the craziest part is he's so young! What am I doing?" I cried.

"Whatever you do, don't tell GQ Boy about this," Tanya advised.

"I'm not that stupid... but what do I do now? Kissing him just makes me want to fuck him."

"Well then, maybe you should fuck him once to get it out of your system," Tanya urged.

"That's exactly what I was thinking. Do you think that would be okay?"

"Just go and have some fun with the kid and leave it at that. You're obviously attracted to him. And Christ, you've already technically cheated on GQ Boy, so I don't know what's stopping you from taking it all the way."

"You know what?! You're absolutely right. I'm gonna fuck him and have some fun and leave it at that," I agreed.

That conversation with Tanya was not to get approval to cheat on GQ Boy, but more to downplay what I was about to do. The entirety of my life was spent in a perpetual uptight manner and for once, I was going to live in the moment which meant I was going to allow myself to enjoy Aiden for one night and after that I would be able to get back on course.

༄

CHAPTER 39

With Christmas fast approaching, it was the perfect opportunity to take advantage of GQ Boy being out of town to have Aiden come over. The day after Christmas, I woke up bright and early to get ready for my date with Aiden. He had accepted my invitation to come over to my place and my plan was to cook him some Vietnamese food. If things went well, then we would end up in bed and by the next day I would be able to get this fling out of my system.

An integral part of my morning was spent grooming myself for the date which included exfoliating, shaving, and moisturizing every inch of my body. Once I was done with that, I gave myself a manicure, pedicure, and scalp treatment to ensure extra-soft hair. The last time I cared to impress a date was with Miguel and my excitable ways brought out the little school girl in me where I wanted to do everything in my power to impress Aiden.

When noon rolled around, I went to the grocery store to pick up some last-minute ingredients I needed for dinner. But once I got home, I felt riddled with guilt. GQ Boy had been such a generous boyfriend. On Christmas Eve, before he left to see his kids, had given me very expensive diamond earrings and five thousand dollars in cash as my Christmas gift. Now, here I was in the midst of my premeditation to cheat on him. I contemplated on canceling with Aiden but in the end lust won over logic. I went ahead with my deceit.

When Aiden arrived, I greeted him at my front door in a casual pink dress as he embraced me in his arms. I was grateful for my decision to dress casual because Aiden was also casually dressed in jeans and a plaid jacket. Even though there was nothing spectacular about his outfit, I still found it to be perfect because he was wearing it.

"Did you have any problems finding my place?" I asked, masking my jittery nerves.

"No, not at all. You live right by the spa."

"I know. Makes for an easy commute," I laughed nervously.

"Nice place," Aiden commented.

"Thanks. It's kind of small."

"It's so neat and organized."

"I'm a complete neat freak. Can you tell?" I smiled.

"I got you something," he said as he handed me a bag.

"Oh, you didn't have to," I replied, pleasantly surprised.

"Oh, it's just something small."

"Oh my God! You remembered!" I exclaimed as I pulled out a copy of *The Shawshank Redemption.*

"Yeah. Well, you said it was your favorite movie. I hope you like it," he said, blushing.

"I love it! Thank you. How was your Christmas?" I asked.

"It was good. It was the same as every year. Just spent it with my family... and you?"

"Same as you. Just spent it with my family," I answered. "Do you still live at home or are you out on your own?" I realized there wasn't much I knew about Aiden.

"I still live at home but I'm planning on moving in with my brother," Aiden answered as he leaned in close and planted his lips on mine.

Those lips sent shock waves of tingles throughout my body, leaving any preconceived notions of his youth aside and before long we had moved onto my sofa, making out savagely like two horny teenagers. He continued to ravage my mouth with his tongue, occasionally stopping to fondle my breasts, each time leaving me wet and panting for more of him. I unzipped his jeans and let my hands explore his package and was pleasantly surprised by his well-endowed size. I slithered my body off the couch, making myself comfortable on the floor, and placed his penis inside my mouth as he let out loud moans of appreciation. It wasn't getting as hard as I wanted, so I worked it a little faster.

Is he gay?

As if he was reading my mind, Aiden blurted out, "I'm so sorry. I'm just really nervous. This has never happened before."

"It's okay. You don't have to be nervous with me. Let's go to my room," I said as I guided him. "Do you have a condom?" I asked, testing him to see if he came prepared.

"No, I don't. I'm sorry. I didn't know what to expect today and I was running late, so I didn't pick any up," he responded nervously.

Luckily I picked some up earlier.

"Well, what do you think would happen when a twenty-eight-year-old woman asks you to come over to her place?" I teased seductively.

As I reached into my end table to pull out a condom, Aiden rushed to open it. He placed it on his now rock-hard penis and swiftly pushed himself inside of me. *It felt amazing!*

Is this for real? How can a twenty-year-old be this good in bed?

Aiden and I went at it for a good while before he collapsed on top of me but within five minutes he was ready for round two. His stamina was like the energizer bunny and his vitality was undeniable in the way that he was able to toss me around and maneuver me into any position with so much ease. He was better than most older men with years of experience which made me question if this was the reason why older men opted to date younger women because it was clear to me now why an older woman would date a younger guy. Maybe it was the sheer fact that I was so ridiculously attracted to him that made the sex so explosive, but regardless of what it was, I wanted more of it.

"C'mon, let me make you dinner now. Are you hungry?" I asked, out of breath after our third time.

"Yeah, I can eat," he replied, trying to catch his breath as well.

I got up and put on my matching lace bra and panties and was about to put on my dress when Aiden requested, "I want you to cook for me in your underwear." I happily obliged.

"Stop it! You're distracting me," I giggled as Aiden tenderly caressed me while I tried to grill the lemon grass chicken and boil the vermicelli noodles.

"I can't believe you're making this dish from scratch. It's my favorite. I always order this when I go to the restaurants," he said in amazement.

"I told you I can cook," I replied while I plated the food into a bowl and served it to him.

We sat there eating dinner and in between bites of food, shared kisses with one another – something I would normally view as pathetically sick, but with Aiden it felt so inviting. The mutual affection from Aiden soothed any doubts in my mind and authenticated the extreme connection sizzling between us and, once again, I found myself transfixed.

"That was so delicious! Thanks for dinner," Aiden said, pulling me in close for another kiss.

"I'm glad you liked it," I beamed.

"You're like the most perfect girl. You're super smart and successful and you can also cook. Not to mention you're really good in bed ..."

"Stop it. You're making me blush," I laughed.

"Is there anything you can't do?" he joked.

"Sure, there's lots of things. And I have a lot of bad qualities as well."

"Like what? I don't believe you."

"Trust me, I do!" I grinned as I caught myself off guard and asked, "Do you want to spend the night with me?

Damn, I need more of him! It's just one night.

"Sure, I'd love to!" he asserted.

"Do you have to work tomorrow?"

"No, I get two weeks off for the Christmas break. I don't go back to work until after the New Year."

"That's awesome. I'm leaving tomorrow to go to Victoria. I'll be spending New Year's there," I said, all of a sudden feeling slightly bummed.

"Well, I'll miss you but can I see you when you get back?" he asked sweetly.

"Sure," I replied, not wanting to tell him that tonight was a one-time thing.

"I want to smoke pot!" I blurted out of the blue.

What? Where did that come from?

"You do?" Aiden asked, surprised. "Do you smoke it often?"

Not since my pot growing days with Tanya.

"No. Only once in a blue moon. But I don't have any. Do you have some?"

"I actually do," he replied, walking over to his jacket to pull out a small plastic bag.

Of course he does. He's twenty!

"Do you smoke a lot of weed?" I asked as I watched Aiden roll a joint like a pro.

"Yeah, I smoke it quite a bit."

Just as I was inhaling the joint, my phone rang.

Shit! That must be GQ Boy! If I don't answer it, he'll think something's wrong and keep calling.

"Excuse me. I need to answer that," I said apprehensively as I left the room.

"Hi, my princess," GQ Boy said.

Shit! Why is he being so sweet?

"Hi," I replied calmly. "How was your Christmas? How are your kids?"

"They're good. Christmas was nice. I miss you..."

Seriously, why is he being so nice? I'm such a bitch for doing this to him.

"Well, I miss you too. So you'll be driving back in the morning and then we're leaving tomorrow night?" I asked confirming our plans.

"Yes, that's right. Have a good night. Sleep tight."

"You too," I said.

"Who was that?" Aiden asked as soon as I walked back into the room.

"That was my boyfriend," I blurted out without even thinking.

"You have a boyfriend!?" he asked, surprised.

Oh shit!

"Yes, I do. He's also my business partner. The one I'm opening the spa with. Our relationship is complicated," I answered, manipulating the truth to justify my dishonor. "Anyway, I don't want to get into too much detail about it. You don't care, do you?"

"I guess not," Aiden replied hesitantly. "Are you going to Victoria with him?"

"Yes, but let's just forget about him. C'mon," I said as I led him back into the bedroom.

To say the least, there wasn't a whole lot of sleeping that night as we spent the majority of the time sexing, with each time being just as incredible as the first. My plan of a one-time tryst had completely backfired and I knew I was in deep trouble.

I needed more of what Aiden was giving, and the thought of never seeing him again made me experience a pain in my chest – another old emotion that I thought I had buried for good. I had taken a bite out of the forbidden apple and there was no turning back.

CHAPTER 40

❧

BOARDING THE PLANE WITH GQ Boy felt so contrite. My previous night's actions left remorse dangling all over me. The strange thing about feeling guilty is that it magnifies the gestures that your boyfriend typically does for you such as opening doors or carrying your bags, to something much bigger. Even though these actions are something you're accustomed to and normally wouldn't think twice about, somehow, after you've cheated, they've become such sweeping gestures. I was bludgeoned with a gut-wrenching pain every time I had to look at GQ Boy and the thought of having to spend New Year's with him made me cringe out of sheer disgrace. Even so, I had to act my best to maintain a level of normalcy because there was no way I was going to leak any truth to him.

"Why are you so tired?" GQ Boy asked as soon as we settled into his Victoria house.

"Oh, I'm just so stressed out about the grand opening of the spa and I haven't been able to sleep very well," I lied, covering up the fact that I was sleep deprived and incredibly sore down there from all the fornication. "Listen... I'm just going to go to bed."

As exhausted as I was, I couldn't fall asleep because my mind was on Aiden and how much I already missed him. With my cell phone an arm's length away, it was easy enough to call Aiden. GQ Boy and I stopped sleeping in the same room a few months after dating. I was an exceptionally light sleeper and GQ Boy's snoring would keep me up at night, so our solution was to sleep in separate bedrooms.

Why do I miss him so much? It hasn't even been twenty-four hours. I just want to hear his voice.

Eventually my body succumbed to my fatigue and I fell into an unruly sleep. I found myself in a recurring dream, running from an unknown force directly into blackness and then suddenly I was freefalling off a cliff into the abyss and just when it seemed that I was nearing the gates of hell, I woke up in a startled sweat.

That's so strange. Normally I never fall off the cliff. I usually stop myself on time. What does this mean? Is it a warning?

I dragged my sluggish body to the kitchen to find GQ Boy making breakfast for us and his sweet affection made me scream inside.

Stop being so nice to me! I don't deserve this. I'm the bitch that cheated on you!

"What do you want to do today?" GQ Boy asked warmly.

"Let's go downtown and do some shopping," I suggested.

"Sure," GQ Boy replied.

Aghhhh! Why do you always give me my way?

After breakfast, my heart froze in excitement when I came back to my room to discover a missed call from Aiden.

"Hi... did you call?" I asked.

"Yeah, I wanted to talk to you. I know you're with your boyfriend but I can't help it... is it okay? He's not standing right by you, is he?"

"No it's fine. I mean it's okay. I miss you like crazy."

Those words escaped from my mouth before I could even compose my emotions and before long the floodgates opened as I uncharacteristically poured my heart out. "I can't get you out of my mind. This is crazy. I mean we just met. You must think I'm some kind of clingy girl."

What is happening to me? I'm losing control of everything!

"No, I don't. I feel the same way you do. I haven't stopped thinking about you since I left your place. I wanted to call you ten minutes after I left. What's worse is that I wish I was there with you and not him," Aiden replied.

He does like me. He's just as crazy about me as I am of him.

"Are you crying?" he asked. "Don't cry. Is it something I said?"

"No, it's not. I don't know why I'm so emotional right now. All I know is that I don't want to be here. I just want to be with you. I really don't know what's happening to me. I don't even know why I'm crying," I sobbed quietly, not wanting GQ Boy to hear me.

"I know this is so crazy but I feel the exact same way. Don't cry, okay? We'll see each other when you get back. It's only a few more days," he said.

Knowing I would see Aiden in a few days cheered me up long enough for me to get through the remainder of the trip. I even managed to enjoy New Year's Eve while fine dining over candlelight to the sounds of a jazz band. At midnight GQ Boy locked me in a tight embrace and whispered tenderly in my ears, "I love you," as he planted a kiss on my lips. I was GQ Boy's Achilles tendon and I knew I was the only person capable of making this man bleed. It wasn't my slightest intention to hurt him in any manner. The unfortunate part was that GQ Boy happened to be an innocent bystander caught in the crossfire of my karmic retribution to all the men I'd hurt.

CHAPTER 41

ॐ

"Oh my God. I've missed you," I expressed as I salaciously continued to make out with Aiden.

"I missed you too," Aiden replied while ripping off my dress.

"I shouldn't be doing this, you were supposed to be a one-night stand," I quivered in ecstasy while Aiden planted his lips all over my body.

"Well it's too late to say that now," Aiden replied.

"I guess I just feel bad," I said. "You know… for what I'm doing."

"It's too late for that, too," Aiden responded, continuing to pleasure me.

Shit! What am I doing? He's got me hooked. He feels so good.

Aiden and I continued our intense affair over the next month. In record time, Aiden broke through my protective cloak that had been shielding me from life's harm. Any notion that love didn't exist was absolved. With Aiden, love existed in such a bespoken way that I couldn't live without him. Just as I needed air to breathe and food to eat, I needed Aiden's sex like none other. At times I acknowledged that the feelings could be that of infatuation. But intuitively I knew it was so much more. I felt like my connection with Aiden was one that transcended time and space. Once I exposed my heart to Aiden, it felt like I had known him beyond this life.

I stopped trying to make sense of our age gap because I had no answer for it. You can't reason with your heart because the heart does not reason, it only feels. Only the mind tries to reason. Despite how much your mind argues with your heart, in the end the heart will always win. Human beings are programmed to make decisions based on emotions and not logic.

For the first time since Miguel, I allowed myself to feel so deeply with Aiden. When we both uttered those three words— 'I love you'—to one another, it cemented the longingness I'd been searching for. Someone did indeed love me but, more importantly, I was capable of reciprocating that love. I was in fact human after all, despite my robotic instincts to shun away love.

Sex could be used as a weapon or it could be used to heal. The majority of my life, I'd used sex as a weapon to control and manipulate men because Uncle Quinn had used sex as a weapon to destroy me. Intimacy with Aiden was the beginning of my sexual healing because I was able to lose myself in the process of our lovemaking and not feel so dirty from it. I was able to explore new sexual territories with Aiden and finally make the connection that when you love someone, the sex with your partner is so much more profound.

CHAPTER 42

꾸

THE DAYS LEADING UP TO the spa's opening were tremendously stressful. I was consumed with every minute detail of the spa to ensure nothing but absolute perfection. Between training the new staff and taking care of last-minute marketing materials, there was so much to do. Even though I was well-prepared and organized, certain things couldn't be done until the end. Even with Carmen's help, it seemed like we were racing against time. When the spa finally opened, I had fallen back on my old nasty habit of smoking to relieve my stress. This made me feel like the biggest hypocrite. I was trying to sell a healthy lifestyle, but my lack of sleep and substitution of cigarettes for food was anything but that. I also enforced a strict 'no smoking' policy with my staff. But I was a closet smoker, which made me a complete fraud.

The morning before the spa opened, I woke up especially early. I felt pangs of anxiety. I stood by my balcony door and lit up a menthol cigarette and immediately felt soothed by the nicotine. I stood staring at the blanket of white that covered the buildings from the previous night's snowfall and with the cool January temperature I could see my breath with each exhale. I should have felt ecstatic because I had been waiting for this moment for three years, but instead I was terrified.

What if nobody shows up today? Well, we already have some appointments, so that's not too bad, I guess. What if nobody shows up the day after? What if the spa is a complete failure?

"You'll do great today. The spa will do great," Aiden assured me as he interrupted my thoughts and wrapped himself around me.

"I hope so," I replied, taking another drag of smoke. "I'm nervous."

"Well, don't be," Aiden said gently. "Will GQ Boy be there today?"

"Yes," I answered. I was slightly agitated being reminded of the added stress of my personal life.

"Sorry for asking," Aiden retorted. "But you know at some point you have to decide between him or me."

"I know, but first I need to focus on getting through today," I snipped.

"Well, can I at least take you out to dinner tonight to celebrate?" Aiden asked.

"I can't... I'm having dinner with GQ Boy," I said sheepishly.

"I know you're feeling stressed today but I'm telling you... I don't know how much more of this I can handle... all this sneaking around. I never thought that I would fall in love with my dream girl and be stuck in a situation like this," Aiden whined. "I'm not saying you have to make a decision today, but soon."

"I know and I will," I replied.

The first day of business went by without much hiccup. I had the staff run a full day's dress rehearsal a few days prior. I did my best to keep my energy high and lead in a positive manner. By the end of the day, while I was in my office doing paperwork, GQ Boy came in with a beautiful bouquet of flowers.

"I'm so proud of you," he marveled.

"Thank you," I replied, taking in the sweet smell of lilies. "We're booked the next few days but nothing much next week. I'm a little worried."

"Don't be. It'll take some time to build up the business. Most businesses don't start making money until after three years. They'll be some growing pains but that's just the nature of business," GQ Boy advised.

Having GQ Boy around always calmed me. I loved that he was older and more experienced when it came to business. He gave me security in all aspects of my life. I knew he would always take care of me as long as I was his. It only made logical sense that I ended things with Aiden once and for all and stay with GQ Boy. Aiden couldn't provide for me financially the way GQ Boy could and one couldn't live on love alone. Ultimately, I made the painstaking decision to break up with Aiden because my ego was relentless in reminding me that being with him was too high of a risk.

The following week, amidst a crazy day of dealing with signage and Valentine's Day promotions, I found a few minutes to call Aiden.

"Hi. Can you talk?" I asked, feeling intense sadness.

"Yeah, what's up?"

"I don't think we should see each other anymore," I blurted out, not knowing how to say it to make it any less painful.

"Are you serious?" he asked.

"Well, you told me to make a decision and I need to focus on my spa. I've worked so hard for it and I don't want to lose it. My situation is complicated with my business partner also being my boyfriend. You know that."

"So it's all about money, isn't it?!" he said, raising his voice.

"No, it's not all about money," I lied. "You're twenty and I'm twenty-eight. We're just in two different places in life. What you want now is not what you're going to want five years from now."

"I don't care about five years from now. All I know is that I love you and I want to be with you right now. I need you."

"I can't keep doing this. I can't keep seeing you and continue a relationship with him and run my spa at the same time. It's impossible! My mind is going crazy right now!" I sobbed.

"Sorry to have upset you," Aiden said, trying to calm me down. "I honestly thought that you were going to choose me over him. I'm not ready to give up on this. You can't cut me out of your life. I'll be more patient, okay? Break up with him when you're ready because I'm not going anywhere."

Oh my God! This is impossible.

"How are you so sure you love me?" I asked.

"Because this feels different from any relationship I've been in. I think about you all the time. You're constantly on my mind. I want to spend every waking second with you. We have the most amazing sex ever! I'm crazy about you," Aiden told me. "And you? You tell me you love me and now you want to break up. How can you say you love me?"

"Believe me, I do. You're the only one who has managed to turn my world upside down and make me feel like I have absolutely no control of my life."

CHAPTER 43

ONE MORNING WHILE GETTING READY for work, I answered GQ Boy's call with the intent of updating him on the progress of the spa. He'd been away for two weeks on a business trip. I made the most of it by having Aiden over every night. A new business is like a baby where it requires your full attention; however, after my botched breakup with Aiden, my attention was consumed with him even moreso. What I should have been doing was focus on generating more business for the spa. However, most of my time was spent covering my tracks because that's what happens when you cheat.

"How was your trip?" I asked.

"It was good but I missed you. I was thinking I'll stop by the spa tonight and we can go for dinner."

"Okay," I replied, holding back tears.

Why am I feeling so emotional?

"How's the spa doing?"

"It's kind of slow. I'm doing the best I can," I replied, bursting into tears.

No, I'm not.

"What's wrong?" GQ Boy asked, concerned.

"Oh, it's nothing," I sobbed. "I'm just really stressed with the spa and I haven't really been sleeping."

Because I stay up all night fucking my brains out.

"Well then, maybe you should take the day off and just sleep and take care of yourself."

I can't do this anymore.

"I think we should break up!" I cried out in pain, releasing all the guilt that had built up inside me in the past couple of months.

"What? What do you mean we should break up? What's going on?" GQ Boy asked.

"Nothing. I haven't felt connected to you for a while and I just need to fully concentrate on the spa. I don't want to be in a relationship right now," I replied while continuing to cry hysterically. "I think I'm having a mental breakdown."

"I think you just need to get some rest and then you'll feel better. You're talking nonsense right now."

No, I'm not. I'm a lying, cheating bitch and you don't deserve this. You deserve so much better.

"I'm serious about my decision. I hope you'll respect that," I continued.

"Okay, whatever you want," GQ Boy replied, confused by my sudden outburst while in denial of what just happened.

What have I done?!!!

It was a huge oversight on my behalf to snap and break up with GQ Boy. But I felt like I was stuck in a bad dream with my life spiraling out of control right in front of me. Every decision I was making dug me a deeper grave. The ramifications of my choices would soon reveal themselves in the ugliest way and bring out the worst in everyone involved.

CHAPTER 44

It's very hard to juggle a new business when your ex-boyfriend is also your business partner. Before I broke up with GQ Boy, he rarely showed up at the spa, allowing me space and freedom to run the business. However, after our breakup, he would regularly show up with flowers to try and win me back with the same tenacity as when he was fighting to make me his. I incessantly refused his dinner invitations, until one occasion GQ Boy cunningly insisted it was about business and I had no choice but to go. Yet immediately upon arriving at the restaurant, it was apparent that it wasn't about the spa.

"Hi," GQ Boy said softly as he got up to pull out my chair. "I could have picked you up."

"It's okay. I wanted to drive," I replied.

"Listen, I don't know what I've done to upset you so much but whatever it is, I'm sorry. Come back to me and let's forget about all this and start over again. Let me make it up to you," he pleaded.

"You haven't done anything. You've been great," I answered.

"Then why the breakup? Is there someone else?"

"No," I lied.

"Then what is it? Make me understand because I've been playing over and over again in my head. What could have made you leave so suddenly? I can't think of anything besides the fact that there could be someone else."

"I'm so sorry. I didn't mean to hurt you. I didn't mean for any of this to happen," I sobbed.

"It's okay. Whatever it is we can still fix it. Let's go away for the weekend and spend some time together," GQ Boy offered.

"I can't. I have to take care of the spa."

"It's okay. You've got Carmen."

Aaaahhhhh! Just tell him.

"I'm seeing someone else right now," I quivered.

"Who?" GQ Boy asked.

"Aiden," I answered as the tears continued flowing down my cheeks.

"The GC's son? Did you cheat on me with him?" GQ Boy asked.

"No," I lied again.

After a long awkward pause GQ Boy looked me dead in my eyes and said, "I can't bear the thought of you being with anybody else, let alone a little kid. I worked so hard to get you to be mine. I patiently waited by your side until you finally quit escorting. I hated sharing you then and I'm not going to share you now with that boy. Does he know about your past?"

"No."

"And what if he doesn't want to be with you anymore when he finds out? I know what you've done and I still love you. Can you say the same about him?"

"No."

"Well then, maybe you should tell him and see if he still wants to stick around. But I doubt it," he sneered.

"Well, that's between Aiden and me!" I snapped back. "I thought you wanted to discuss business?"

"I'm warning you to choose your next move wisely," GQ Boy said.

My next move should have been to end things with Aiden. Instead, I continued seeing Aiden while ignoring GQ Boy until one morning I received a phone call from GQ Boy. That phone call was inevitable. It shouldn't have come as a shock, but it did rattle me to my core. Up until then, my ego was still making my mind believe that it was possible to have my cake and eat it too.

"I want out of the spa. I can't be business partners with you anymore. It's too hard to deal with you professionally when I'm still in love with you," he said, sounding as if he was choking back tears.

"What? What am I supposed to do? You know I can't carry the spa without you," I yelled.

"Then maybe you should have thought of that before you decided to run off with your little boy toy!" he retorted, flipping his mood from sadness to anger. "You're a cold, heartless bitch. You thought you could just use me to build the spa and then dispose of me like you did with all your exes. Well, I don't have to stick around for this shit and I won't."

"I'm so sorry for hurting you," I cried. "Even though it may look like I used you to build the spa, I didn't. That wasn't my intention."

I didn't anticipate falling in love. This was not how I imagined things to be!

"You probably say that to all of your exes. But I see your true colors now."

"Can we talk about this in person? I mean, we spent so much money on this spa and now you just want to walk away?" I begged.

"Well, I suggest you start looking for other investors. I never wanted to open up a spa. I did it for you because it was your dream! I thought we were life partners. I didn't think you would go and dump me the minute it opened!"

Yes, I'm so stupid!

"And all for what?" he continued. "For a fuckin' boy. A fuckin' kid!"

"I know. You're right," I replied wiping my tears. "Look, I know how much you hate to eat alone. Can we discuss this over dinner?"

"As I see it, you have two options. It's the spa and me or the boy. I hope you make the right decision."

What was I thinking? I wish I'd never met Aiden!

CHAPTER 45

⅌

THE DECISION I HAD TO make was one of love or money. Tanya's stance was clear when she said, "Your situation is like a goddamn reality show. I would always choose love over money because you can always make money. But true love is rare and if you're lucky enough to find it… you don't let it go."

I turned to Beaver, who remained a good friend and confidant, even working on the spa as the computer consultant.

"You're a catch to him," he said. "It's a prize when a younger guy can get an older woman, especially if the older woman is successful and hot. He's got everything to gain and you've got everything to lose. You need to get rid of the kid and stick with GQ Boy. The guy is rich and established. Sure, he's older than you but he's mature and can take good care of you. The kid has nothing to offer you."

I needed to talk to someone who could see both positions and help me rationalize things through. That person was Carmen.

"I was worried this might happen and I tried to warn you," Carmen lectured. "And now here we are. I know it's easy for people standing on the outside to cast judgment and tell you to leave Aiden, but obviously if it was that easy then you would have after that first night. Now that's not saying that I agreed with you cheating on GQ Boy because I don't… but what's done is done. At the same time, I really can't understand your obsession with Aiden. It's like he has a spell on you. Then again, it's not for me to understand…"

"Carmen, you're not helping me," I whined. "What should I do?"

"It's not my decision to make. You have to make this decision. You're about to lose your spa. Do you even care?"

"Of course I care! I don't want to lose it."

"Then break up with Aiden," Carmen encouraged.

"I've tried to break up with Aiden before, but when he calls I'm too weak to stay away from him," I whimpered.

"Is he worth it?" Carmen asked matter-of-factly.

"I love him. I've never felt this way about anyone. He's the one."

"Well then, give up the spa and shut it down. Choose love over money. You've always been one to choose money over love. Now life is putting you in this position to truly test you."

"Or it's karma for all the guys I mistreated," I said.

"Possibly... karma's a bitch. Does Aiden know about your past?"

"No. Do you think I should tell him?"

"I think he deserves to know, especially if you think he's the one. Don't you think he deserves to know so he can make a decision on whether he wants to be with you or not?" Carmen suggested.

"Well, I know he doesn't think highly of street girls. He's always making some crude remark when he sees them standing around."

"Well then, maybe you should tell him. It might make your decision easier. He might not want to be with you after he finds out. But if he truly loves you, then he will love you regardless," Carmen informed.

I'd never been the kind of girlfriend who felt the need to tell their boyfriend everything. Some things were better left unsaid. The thought never crossed my mind to divulge my past to Aiden. I feared he would reject me if he knew, but also that he would expose my secret to others. At the same time, if telling Aiden would help my decision-making process, then I was willing to risk having him disclose my secret.

There isn't exactly a 'best time' to tell your boyfriend: "Hey, I used to be an escort and prior to that I grew marijuana." So I decided I would tell him that evening. If he was going to walk out, then it was better that he did it now.

"What's the worst thing you ever done?" I asked Aiden.

"Nothing really. Maybe sell some drugs at a party," Aiden replied. "What's the worst thing you've ever done?"

"Well, I'm afraid after I tell you, you won't want to be with me," I answered.

"That's ridiculous. There's nothing that you could have done that would make me not want to be with you. Tell me," Aiden insisted.

"I don't know how," I hesitated.

"Just go out and say it!" he urged.

"Well, I guess the worst thing I've ever done was…," I paused.

"Was what?"

"Well, I worked as an escort for over a year," I blurted out.

"You what?!" Aiden exclaimed.

"I was an escort."

"What the fuck!? Why didn't you tell me this sooner?" he gasped.

"Well, it's not exactly something you tell someone when you first meet," I replied.

"I can't believe you didn't tell me this sooner!" he said. "You know how I feel about hookers. I can't fuckin' believe this! You were my dream girl and now everything I thought you were didn't even really exist!"

"Stop it… please listen to me. Let me explain to you how I got into it!" I yelled back. "Not everyone was born with a silver spoon in their mouth like you."

"What does that have to do with this?"

"You had a good start to your life. I didn't. You told me many times how happy your childhood was and all the trips your parents took you on. You come from a perfect family whose parents have lots of money. I didn't grow up like that. My life was tough," I shared.

"It was so tough you had to sell your body for money?" he sneered.

"Yes. And in time, I will try and share more with you. Just believe me when I tell you that I made those decisions at the time out of necessity and desperation. No girl grows up wanting to sell their bodies for a living," I reflected emotionally.

"Is that how you met 'old balls'? Was he a client of yours?"

"Yes."

"So you just used him to get your spa?"

"No. He gave me an opportunity I couldn't refuse and I took it. I was faithful to him the entire time until I met you. We did have a genuine relationship. It's just that I was never in love with him but I treated him with kindness and respect. You have to understand that prior to you I never believed in love."

"I'm still disgusted by 'old balls.' I'm disgusted by anyone who has to pay for sex."

"That's your viewpoint and it's a very short-sighted one. You're young, so you have all the energy in the world to go out and meet girls. When you're older and have a career that consumes most of your time, it's not so easy. I can tell you most of my clients were good people."

"I'm just in shock right now. I'm hurt that you lied to me and I'm repulsed by what you used to do," Aiden answered.

"Look, if you can't see past this and you think I'm a whore, then you should just leave. I can't change what I've done. I wanted to tell you because I do love you and thought that you deserved to know the truth."

Somewhere between all the fighting and crying we both managed to fall asleep. In the morning I awoke to an empty bed with a note from Aiden on my nightstand.

CHAPTER 46

༄

I SAT PATIENTLY WAITING FOR my next interview to show up as my thoughts slowly drifted to the note Aiden left me.

Stay focused. Get through your interviews today and then deal with Aiden later.

I thought that the spa could use a good male therapist. I was expecting a Caucasian guy to show up but when Ade walked into my office, I was taken aback.

"Have a seat," I instructed, trying my best to remain professional and not stare at the beautiful 6'-tall black man standing in front of me.

Wow, it's not every day you see a black massage therapist... and he's hot.

"So I see from your résumé that you just graduated from massage school. Why do you want to work here?" I asked.

"I've heard really good things about this spa. I'm looking to work at a good place and this spa seems to be it," Ade replied.

That's weird. Why won't he look at me in the eyes?

"Okay," I swallowed, my eyes still on him. "What is your availability?"

"I'm available every day. I'm new to the city, so I just want to work and save some money," Ade answered, shifting his gaze to the floor.

He doesn't like to make eye contact.

"Where are you from?" I asked, not taking my eyes off him.

"Toronto," Ade replied, observing the room.

Ah, that explains his good sense of style and those shoes.

"How long do you plan on staying in this city?"

"As long as it takes," Ade responded.

"What do you do in your free time?" I pried, wanting to get a better sense of Ade.

Is that even a valid interview question?

"I read and sleep."

That's kind of boring.

"What kind of books do you read?"

"I read health books. I'm into cleansing and taking herbal supplements."

This guy is so different!

"Okay, well the job is yours if you want it," I offered Ade. "I'll just have to call and check your references and if all goes well, you can start next week."

"Thank you," Ade answered politely.

That's a first. I've never hired anybody on the spot.

"Great!" I exclaimed, reaching out to shake Ade's hand. As he firmly shook my hand, Ade's dark eyes pierced into mine. For a split second, the force behind it was so polarizing that I instantaneously retreated my hand and looked away.

What just happened?!

"Let me show you the spa," I said flustered.

"Who designed the space?" Ade questioned while walking through the spa.

"I did," I replied. "Well, I mean, I envisioned it and hired designers to draw it out," I answered while checking out Ade's perfectly lean physique.

The girls are going to like him.

"You designed this space?" Ade asked. "Hmmm... that means you're a creative person by nature. You have the ability to control your destiny."

"Thanks," I replied.

What does he mean I have the ability to control my destiny? If he only knew what a mess my personal life is.

CHAPTER 47

ℭ

MY PLAN OF TELLING AIDEN about my escorting days in hopes of it making my decision easier had completely backfired. I smoked until I was comatose and when my lungs felt like they were bleeding, I pulled out Aiden's letter and read it again for the umpteenth time.

I love you. I will not give up on us. I'm in too deep.

What am I going to do? Who do I choose? There's millions at stake!

My entire belief system was rattled. This young person just appeared in my life and now threatened the very existence of my survival. No matter how much I tried to intellectualize why life introduced me to Aiden, I couldn't come up with a viable answer. Not once did it occur to me that meeting Aiden could have been the beginning of a possible transformation in my life.

In order to transform your life, one must acknowledge one's unhappiness and indicate a desire to make the necessary adjustments. For so long, I had not recognized my unhappiness because being in that state felt normal to me, so there was no need for change. Aiden made me cognizant of love and the result was joyous, but I still couldn't make the connection that I was undergoing a transformation. I could feel a shift in my paradigm but there was so much happening around me that I couldn't sit still long enough to observe it.

When one's survival feels threatened, one has the instinct to turn to what's safe. In my case, being in a one-sided relationship where I felt no vulnerability was always where I thrived. I made the grueling decision to end it with Aiden for good.

"Aiden, my situation with the spa and GQ Boy is so complicated. As much as I appreciate you still wanting to be with me after what I told you, I think its best that we stop seeing each other," I said solemnly.

"Are you serious?!" Aiden yelled over the phone. "First you drop this escorting shit on me and when I tell you that I still want to be with you… you break up with me? Do you ever stop and think about how I feel? Do I not get a choice in this?"

"GQ Boy has threatened to back out of the spa if I don't get back with him," I cried.

"So he's blackmailing you now? People break up all the time. He needs to grow the fuck up and act like an adult!" Aiden shouted.

"I don't have enough money to carry the costs of the spa. Without his money, then the spa will shut down. It's only a matter of time. We're losing money every month," I confided.

"I thought you said that business was picking up."

"It is, but not quick enough. The spa needs more time to grow and more time means more operating cash. I'm tapped out on my end," I explained.

"Listen to me. You can't do this to us. I love you. I'm begging you… don't give up on us. We're too attached to each other and you know it," Aiden said between sobs. "I can't live without you. I don't want to live without you."

"I know, but I have no choice. I don't want this to end but what else am I supposed to do?" I bawled.

"I fuckin' hate that guy! Are you absolutely sure you want to do this?" Aiden grilled.

"No, but I have no choice. Goodbye. I love you."

That night, I cried like someone had died. It was the worst pain I had felt in my entire life – making what I felt with Miguel seem insignificant. It's the kind of pain that puts you into a fetal position and makes an atheist person call out to God. You beg for mercy and make all sorts of negotiations to be a kinder and more generous person, all so the pain can dissipate. You even welcome physical pain because physical pain will eventually heal whereas the excruciating pain of a tortured heart seems eternal and when the impenetrable loss seeps into your core, no amount of money in the world exonerates it.

ꝏ

IT'S IMPOSSIBLE TO STAY FOCUSED on anything when you're suffering from a broken heart but when it came to training Ade, I tried my best to remain alert. I started as I always did with any massage therapist and had him massage me so I could get a feel for his style. Some therapists spend too much time overthinking the techniques, so the massage could end up too robotic. I look for a unique individual style that each therapist brings to their treatment that makes the client want to return. Even though I can't train a therapist on how to craft a signature way, what I do train them on is how to incorporate company protocols into their treatment to construct the ultimate experience for the client.

What I found astounding about Ade was how he miraculously calmed me into a meditative state, especially when my mind was perpetually hounded by thoughts of Aiden. Outwardly, I was going through all the motions of training Ade, but privately I was mulling over how in such an insanely stressful time in my life, Ade's touch was the only thing that made me feel centered and brought me to a place where I found a moment of peace.

When you're going through a difficult time, you naturally gravitate to a higher energy source as a lifeline to stop you from drowning. It's like a leech that sucks on someone else's blood in order to survive. Metaphorically, you become that leech that needs to tap into someone else's energy source. Usually this is done without any awareness on your behalf which explains why I continued to go to Ade for massages even after our training had ended.

Without me even speaking, Ade already knew that I was in trouble. He was someone with an elevated consciousness that operated on a different level.

It became apparent that Ade was a person of few words, choosing to listen more than to speak. When he did speak, his words were always delivered with an impact that made you examine the complexity of your life due to the deep and philosophical undertone.

"I notice you never eat on your lunch break. How can you go all day massaging and not eat? Don't you feel hungry?" I questioned Ade one evening during one of our massages.

"No, it's about conditioning your mind. I'm cleaning out my body to re-mineralize it."

"But at some point you will start eating more than crackers, right?" I asked jokingly.

"Sure, but it's about eating organic foods that nourish and elevate your energy rather than eating foods that lower your vibration," explained Ade.

"What? I don't understand?" I answered.

"You want to eat plant-based and avoid meat because animals are of the flesh and killing them to consume their meat is like killing life," Ade explained slowly.

"I've never met anyone who thinks like you. You're really into health, aren't you?"

"There's nothing to live for but to be healthy," Ade responded calmly. "People are always in a rush to get from one place to another and the question is: Why? We're all going to die one day and our only job is to try to slow down the death process but people are so unaware; they run around thinking they're doing something when in reality their just rushing to die."

This explains why he does everything so slowly.

"You just described me. I'm always rushing around like a chicken with my head chopped off."

"I know," Ade remarked.

"You do?" I asked, alarmed.

"I'm an observer. I watch people," Ade said as he massaged my temples, putting me at ease.

"What made you become a massage therapist? What did you do in Toronto before coming here?"

"I worked in the film industry as a location scout."

"Wow! The film industry, that sounds glamorous," I commented.

"No, it's not glamorous—long hours—and I didn't enjoy it. I fell into it by accident but that's no industry for a healer like myself. I'm much more suited to working as a massage therapist."

"Well, I do agree there's something about being around you that's so nurturing. I can't really explain it, but these massages that you've been giving me have helped me feel so rested. You must think I'm crazy."

"No, I understand. That's what healers do with touch. It's the transfer of energy coming from a higher vibe to a lower vibe," Ade illustrated.

"I don't understand," I replied.

"You will one day. When you see... you can't unsee."

When you see you can't unsee? What is he talking about?!

"You're an old soul," I remarked. "You're very wise for a thirty-one-year-old. I wish I had as much insight as you."

I wouldn't be in the mess I'm in now.

"Don't ever envy anyone. I wouldn't wish my life upon anybody."

And you wouldn't want mine neither.

"Then why be a healer? Why not something else?" I inquired.

"You don't choose to be a healer. Life makes that choice for you. I've been healing people ever since I was born. Trust me when I say it's a thankless job. People only call me in their darkest hours and when things are good again they disappear," Ade responded, letting out a long sigh.

"So people just come to you in their troubled times without even knowing why?" I asked perplexed.

"Yes."

"I don't believe that! They must know why they're calling you!" I exclaimed.

"Not consciously. That's why you're here," Ade said.

What?!

"No," I denied.

Is he mind-fucking with me?

"Whatever it is you're going through, remember… everything passes in life and this too shall pass because nothing is permanent. The only permanent thing is impermanency itself," Ade enlightened.

CHAPTER 49

⚘

GQ BOY EASED UP ON his pressure once I told him that things were over between Aiden and me and gave me the space that I pleaded for. I wasn't ready to run back into GQ Boy's arms but he made it clear that so long as I wasn't with Aiden, he was okay to leave me alone to run the spa. It gave me comfort knowing that my spa still had a chance. On the other hand, it did nothing to remedy the constant pain of my aching heart. All it took was one phone call from Aiden to eradicate all the positive reinforcement that I had been feeding myself about making the right decision.

"Hello?" I answered, my heart pounding.

"Hi. It's me. How are you?" Aiden asked.

"I'm terrible," I answered, the tears welling up in my eyes.

"Why?" he asked, concerned.

"Because my heart is broken!" I wailed, letting all the tears explode.

"Don't cry. My heart is broken, too."

"I thought I made the right decision and I've tried to remain strong, but hearing your voice now…"

"I know," Aiden interrupted. "I can't sleep or eat. I've missed work this week because I was so sad I couldn't even get out of bed. I need to see you tonight. Can I see you tonight?"

"Yes," I agreed without hesitation because I was *that* weak when it came to Aiden.

When he arrived, Aiden said, "We're going to be together. The last week without you has been torture. I don't ever want to feel that way again.

There's got to be a way for us to be together," he urged as he planted kisses on my lips.

"I know. I felt so miserable all week, too. I don't want to be apart from you. I really don't know what to do," I replied, barbarically biting his lips for more.

"Did you tell 'old balls' that we broke up?" Aiden inquired, groping me all over.

"Yes, I told him a couple of days ago," I answered while all over Aiden.

"Well then, just let him keep thinking that. The only reason he wants to pull the plug on the spa is because he found out about us. If he keeps thinking that we're over, then he'll leave you alone."

"Okay," I replied as I hungrily tore open Aiden's pants. As things heated up, we were interrupted by my phone.

"Shit, it's 'old balls'!" I panicked.

"Don't answer it!" Aiden snarled.

"If I don't answer it, he'll keep calling," I replied, answering the call.

"It's me. I'm at your front door. Open up!" GQ Boy yelled.

"What are you doing here? I told you I wasn't feeling well!" I snapped back.

"I know that little shit is up there. Let me in!" he persisted. "I'm coming in one way or another."

Fuck! I'm so busted.

With my heart racing frantically and my mind a blank, without thinking, I buzzed him in.

"Shit! He's here. I just fuckin' buzzed him in by accident. You need to get out of here now!" I yelled.

"Shit!" Aiden shouted as he bolted for the door, grabbing his shoes and jacket on the way out.

Please, dear God, don't let them run into each other!

"I saw your fuckin' boy toy sprint for the stairs like the boy that he is! What? He couldn't stay and face me? Have a real conversation with me like a man? That's right! He's fuckin' twenty years old!" GQ Boy screamed.

"You lied to me. You told me you two were over and you're still seeing him. Did you ever really break up with him?" he continued yelling. "Well, if you want to be with him, then I suggest you go and find a new business partner because

I'm done. I want out of the spa and if you can't get another investor, then the spa will shut down. I can't believe you're giving this all up for a fuckin' kid!" GQ Boy said.

I looked shamefully to the ground and cried not knowing what to do. I was at a loss for words because in the years that I've known GQ Boy, I've never witnessed him so angry. When I finally composed myself, all I managed to say was: "If you're going to shut down the spa, then just shut it down."

"Well then, say goodbye to your spa," GQ Boy said.

"Just get out of here!" I screamed. "Leave me the fuck alone!"

I slammed the door in his face and ran into my room burying my face deep into the pillow, hoping to suffocate myself.

AAAAHHHHHH!!!! I JUST WANT TO DIE!

CHAPTER 50

༄

WITH GQ BOY'S INHERENT THREAT looming over me, I continued to show up at the spa waiting for the inevitable to happen. Amidst the chaos, once again, I gravitated towards Ade without understanding why his presence captivated me. Normally when I'm drawn to someone, it's usually the result of a physical attraction. Even though I recognize Ade to be very handsome, mine was more of a spiritual attraction.

I had a gut-wrenching instinct that Ade was someone I could confide in. In retrospect, because I don't believe in coincidences, I know Ade was sent into my life at a pertinent time to guide me through my darkest moments. I was on the verge of what I thought was an emotional collapse, but it was so much more than that. I was a spiritually broken human being and in need of a transformation in order to heal myself.

"Ade, the spa is not doing well and I'm not in a good place," I disclosed.

"I know. But I already told you… this too shall pass," Ade spoke.

"I'm afraid I'm going to lose everything," I uttered while Ade massaged my back.

"You can't lose anything because there's nothing to lose," Ade replied.

"I don't understand," I said.

"You can only lose something that you think you had ownership to. As long as you put a stake on it, there will always be some kind of attachment. Can you enjoy without attachment and know when to die to it? That's the problem with the human ego. It wants to own everything and never knows when to lay something to rest."

"I wanted to build something extraordinary... I wanted to become extraordinary," I confessed, changing the topic as I still couldn't grasp what Ade was conveying.

"Extraordinary... well, that means extra-ordinary. Do you mean to say that being ordinary isn't good enough? That you have to be extra in order to be better? That ordinary things are not enough to capture beauty and only if it has extra qualities will it shine above the rest? Well, I hate to break it to you but *all* beauty lies in the ordinary for in the ordinary is where beauty lies."

"You've lost me." I flatly said.

"If you want to be extraordinary like you said, then you need to go inside yourself to discover what it is that makes you extra-ordinary. Relying on outward achievements will never quench your thirst because once you acquire it, there'll be something else and something else. It's like being stuck in a revolving door wanting to escape but not knowing how. Is there anything extraordinary about the revolving door? No. The extraordinary thing is to be the observer of the door and not the one trapped in it."

"So, it's better to stand back and observe than to be stuck in the cycle. Is that what you're trying to say?" I asked.

"Yes. And in order to be the observer, you must go inside to find the answers because it's damn cold outside and I don't know about you but I'd rather be warm," Ade chuckled, lightening up the mood.

"I like your analogies," I laughed. "It makes me think."

"That's the whole point."

"How do I begin this inward journey? Where do I start?" I asked.

"You start by dying to everything you've ever known or thought you knew," Ade answered. "It'll be the hardest journey you'll ever embark on, and most people will never take this journey. But if you do, you will completely transform your life and your reality."

"Is that what you mean when you told me I had the ability to control my destiny?"

"Yes, but the question is... are you ready for this transformation? Are you ready to dissect every aspect of your life, no matter how uncomfortable, to understand the very core of who you are? Your deepest and darkest fears will surface and there will be nowhere to hide. If you can do that, then you can customize the future that you want."

"That seems like it can take a while and right now I need something along the lines of a new investor or influx of cash."

"There you go again. Can't you see that relying on the external world to solve your problems is like putting a Band-Aid on a wound that needs surgery? There's no quick fixes or shortcuts. You're either going to do the work or end up stuck in the revolving door unable to escape your misery. Most people spend their lives stuck in that revolving door. The question is... are you going to be the observer or the one that's trapped? Only you can decide."

Of course I wanted to be the observer. But the question was 'how' when all the drama in my life was the focal point of my universe.

CHAPTER 51

꼬

THE LOVE TRIANGLE BETWEEN AIDEN, GQ Boy, and me escalated to an all-time high and had me stuck in an emotional rollercoaster. GQ Boy was dialing me almost every night drunk. Each time, he conveyed different sentiments because he was mourning the loss of our relationship. I should have been more patient with him. After all, I was the cause of his heartache. But I was furious every time we spoke because I just wanted him out of my life.

"So you left me for a fuckin' kid, hey?" GQ Boy shouted.

"You're fuckin' drunk! Why are you calling me?" I asked.

"Well, I just wanted to talk to you," he said, slurring his words.

"How much have you had to drink?"

"I've only had a few drinks."

"Bullshit! You're shit-faced!" I yelled.

"No, I'm not!" he replied, continuing his slur.

"What do you want?" I asked.

"So you're going to choose the kid over the spa?"

"He's not a kid! He happens to be very mature for his age," I said.

"Right. How old is he again?" GQ Boy sneered.

"Okay, so what? Why the fuck are you still calling me if we broke up and you're shutting down the spa? Leave me the alone."

"Well, you're the one who doesn't want to leave the kid. You made that decision very clear when you decided to sneak behind my back and continue seeing him," GQ Boy quipped. "I'm going to fuckin' destroy you!"

"You're going to destroy me? How are you going to do that?" I asked.

"Does he know you used to be an escort? I'm going to tell him what you used to do!"

"I already told him. Save yourself the trouble," I snipped.

"I don't believe you. Maybe I'll call him up right now," GQ Boy devised.

"Go ahead. He'll just tell you to fuck off!" I screamed.

Another evening, GQ Boy called me enraged and threatened to sue me personally, stating, "I'll see to it that you file personal bankruptcy and then you're going to have to move back home with your parents. I'll make sure you don't have a penny to your name and you'll live the remainder of your life in misery!"

On another occasion, I got the crying drunk when he professed, "You broke my heart. After everything I've done for you. I fuckin' made you. I got you out of escorting and gave you the life that you have. How can you do this to me? I love you so much."

To make matters worse, GQ Boy's phone calls always riled Aiden and I would get an earful from him saying, "He's lucky I respect senior citizens because if he wasn't so old I'd beat the shit out of him."

"Stop it. He's heartbroken... he's not normally like this. People act out of character when they're hurt," I explained, fighting for GQ Boy.

"Why do you always defend 'old balls'?

"Because I know he's a good man. He's hurt and I'm the bitch that did this to him," I quietly replied.

It was safe to say that they both despised each other. As our love triangle dragged on, it only deepened the turmoil that was brewing inside me. I knew that both GQ Boy and Aiden were wonderful people caught up in unwanted circumstances. I was the lousy person who put the three of us in that predicament, so I deserved to be the one to hear the wrath from both parties.

CHAPTER 52

߷

"WHY ARE RELATIONSHIPS SO DIFFICULT?" I asked Ade during another massage session.

"It's only hard because people have unrealistic expectations of them," Ade answered.

"Then they're bound to fail?" I questioned.

"A true relationship is when two people are on the same wavelength in the exact space and time... only then can it be harmonious. The unfortunate part is that it rarely happens; therefore, most relationships are doomed from the get go," Ade explained.

"But what if you are on the same wavelength and it still doesn't work out?"

"Then you never were together in that exact moment. Rather, you were in a relationship with a snapshot or image of that reality."

"You've lost me," I replied.

"People have the tendency to project onto the other person the ideal image of their partner and if that partner fails to live up to that snapshot then they get upset. How can a relationship truly exist when two people are projected images? Where in that lies the true self?"

"Well, if that's the case, then what's the point of relationships? Why are people always on the quest to be in relationships?" I asked.

"Relationships have their importance in that it reflects your state of being in that moment in time. It acts as a psychological mirror that allows you to see the subjective aspect of yourself," Ade explained.

"Hypothetically speaking, if an older person is dating a much younger person, does that mean that the older person is in some way emotionally stumped? And that's a reflection of where they are emotionally?" I asked, thinking of Aiden and GQ Boy.

"That means that somewhere along the way, the person has relinquished their will for any self-discovery and this can arise from trauma, a bad breakup, a death. So they dwindle their capacity to self-actualize. When any of their relationships come to an end, that's when the true nature of their emotional maturity surfaces."

Does that mean I've got the emotional maturity of a fifteen-year-old because I had been so scarred from Miguel and now Aiden represents lost love? What about GQ Boy? What do I represent to him?

"I see," I reflected.

"Relationships shape and define your existence. In relationships, all things come to be. The description is not to describe, "Ade informed.

The description is not to describe. What does that mean?

"Would you say that there's a lot of ego involved in relationships? If we let go of our egos, then relationships have a better chance of survival?" I asked, changing the topic.

"Ego and you are one of the same. It's not a separate identity like most scholars think. There's nothing wrong with ego if it's in its proper place. What is ego but an accumulation of memories based on a degree of knowledge? Keep in mind, with knowledge, ego feels a need to control and own. It becomes detrimental when people tie their personal identities to their ego and when their ego is challenged, they will defend it to their death because it's a direct threat to how they view the world."

Holy shit! How could I have been so blind?

CHAPTER 53

ჭ

IF YOUR EMOTIONS STEM FROM your heart, my mind was a bi-product of my ego which, based on Ade's theory, was an accumulation of twenty-eight years of knowledge. I was one of those people who tied their identities to their ego. When I made the decision to be with Aiden, I challenged my ego because all these years I repeatedly told myself that love didn't exist.

My ego had been content living in a pile of manure that any introduction to happiness posed as a threat to its existence. It had to ensure the state of its survival, so it fed me toxic inclinations that I was able to have both the spa and Aiden. In reality, it's ludicrous to believe that I can get away with such deception. If I was a wise person, I would have already foreseen the outcome before it even played out. But I wasn't consciously evolved, so I let my ego manipulate me into believing that I could outsmart the system and curb things to my favor. In the end, the inevitable happened and the spa shut down eight months after it opened.

I'll never forget the day when I had to make the announcement to my staff and hand everyone their last paycheck. Carmen was calm only because she knew what was happening all along, while I can only equate Ade's poise to the sage in him. The rest of the staff received the news in shock. I felt like an utter failure and retreated to my office, leaving Carmen to address any questions.

When the staff all left, I had Carmen and Tanya help me pack up some personal belongings while I took a few minutes to walk around the spa to say my final goodbye. None of it felt real and, in fact, the past eight months felt like a bad dream. I stood waiting for my alarm clock to wake me and pick up from when the spa was still in construction. I wanted to rewind back to when GQ Boy and I were together and happy. But the reality was I had single-handedly built and destroyed the spa despite all the warnings from Carmen and Tanya.

I wandered into the gym. *This is where it all began.* I sat down on the treadmill as I did that fateful night when Aiden and I spent hours talking to each other. *If only I could go back to that night and leave things the way they were instead of pursuing him like I did...* But everything was too late now. I ended up with Aiden but why wasn't I happy?

"Are you okay?" Tanya asked as she walked towards me and gave me a hug.

"This is where it all started," I replied as the tears came pouring down my face.

"I know," she said.

"I wish I never met Aiden. I should have listened to you guys but I didn't," I sobbed. "I was on top of the world months ago. How did I go from having it all to having nothing?"

"What you had before was money. Money can always be replaced but love can't. Everything happens for a reason. Listen, just take some time off and pull yourself together. You'll figure out what to do with your life soon enough. You're lucky you still have enough money to take a few months off and not have to worry."

"Yeah, that's if GQ Boy doesn't put me into personal bankruptcy. You know he's threatened that many times."

"I don't think he will. He's just hurt."

"Will I be okay?" I asked weakly.

"You're a fighter. You'll be more than okay. You'll get back up when you're good and ready," Tanya smiled.

"Thanks, girl," I said, wiping the tears with the back of my hands.

But how? How do I move on and recover from this?

STAGE THREE

Transformation

(Acceptance, Forgiveness, and Finally... Love)

CHAPTER 54

ঔ

I SPIRALED INTO A DEEP depression in the weeks that followed and spent most of my time in bed sleeping. When I finally emerged from my sleep coma, I was dead inside, and felt like I had nothing left to contribute to the world. I withdrew from life and refused to leave my condo for months. My family, Tanya, and Aiden were very sensitive towards my despair and respected my wishes of wanting to be left alone, only checking in on me occasionally.

I had hit rock bottom and had no sense of self. Many times I found myself lying on my floor staring up at the ceiling wanting to cry or scream but nothing escaped – I was an empty vessel. There in me lied remnants of a hollow carcass, a former self that was defined by egotistical ambitions, caught in a web of self-absorption, which led to my ultimate demise.

After months of self-loathing, I came to the conclusion that the good thing about hitting rock bottom is that there's only two possible outcomes. You can stay on the floor and continue to stare at the ceiling for the remainder of your life, or you could stand up and start walking again. Being at the bottom means there's nowhere else to go but up.

Ade once told me, 'once you see, you can't unsee' and those words always struck a chord with me. If the collectiveness of my life has been nothing but me stumbling around in the dark, then I was ready to step into the light and seek truth. Something inside of me was urgently telling me that I needed to change and that I couldn't continue on the way I had before. You can lie to yourself, but you can't lie to life because life has a way of sending you messages to tell you that you are spiritually broken. It's like your alarm clock ringing to alert you and there's only so many times you can press snooze before the ringing becomes deafening. I knew it was time to make a transformation or else I would end back up like my fifteen-year-old self in the hospital, only this time the outcome would be fateful.

I turned to Ade for guidance. As much as I hated going to therapy before, talking to Ade was very much like therapy because it helped me externalize my problems. Ade was very unobtrusive, never probing me to share what I didn't want to, and by doing so I found myself divulging personal details about my life to him which was more than I had done with any previous therapist.

"How are you holding up?" Ade asked when we met up for tea on one of the rare occasions that I went out.

"I don't know," I answered. "I'm a mess most of the time but occasionally I have my strong moments. I know I have a lot of emotional issues I need to deal with. The only thing is, I don't know how. Where do I even begin?"

"Don't focus too much on the how. Start by cleaning out your body. Your only job right now is to take care of your health," Ade encouraged.

"Ade, how are you so wise? You're wise beyond your years," I said.

"Listen. I'm an old soul. I feel like I've walked this Earth ten times over. You need to go inside yourself to find the answers. Don't rely on the external world for anything because it's constantly shifting. The spa shutting down was bound to happen. I knew from the moment I walked in for my interview."

"How did you know?" I asked.

"Because it was your energy. You carried around a very dense energy full of sorrow and hatred. It was bound to collapse. I didn't even want to take the job because I wanted nothing to do with that energy."

"Then why did you take the job?"

"Lina, I'm telling you, you're my last one. I've been nursing people through death my whole life and all I wanted to do was show up at the spa and make my money. Then I run into you."

"What do you mean you've been nursing people through death your whole life?"

"Lina, you don't understand. I'm not the fun guy. I'm not the guy who gets all the girls. I'm the guy people call when their life is falling apart and they need to have a real conversation. I've helped so many people through the worst parts of their lives. I've been doing that my entire life and I swore to myself that I was done with all that."

"Then why help me?"

"Because I have no choice. Life brought us together for a reason. But you're my last one, I swear. I don't have the energy anymore to heal anyone else. It's a thankless job."

"Well, I'm grateful for your friendship."

"Listen. Let me break it down slowly to you because I don't want to overwhelm you all at once. The spa shutting down was no coincidence. It had nothing to do with you, GQ Boy, or little buddy there. Any unresolved emotional issues from your past need to be dealt with or else this will continue to happen again. The next time you build something, it will collapse. The only difference is the people in the story will be different."

"So do you think these issues could have manifested as far back as my childhood?" I asked.

"Absolutely, because who you are today is a direct impact of how you grew up. Get to the root of those issues and resolve it."

"You make it seem so easy. Like there's a handbook I can buy to help me with my fucked up childhood. See, the health stuff is the easy part. There's plenty of health books I can buy, but there's no handbook to help me resolve my childhood issues," I said, getting all worked up.

"Then for now, just focus on your health. Trust me, you'll have so much more clarity when you have a healthy body to work with," Ade said. "When you're ready, things will reveal themselves."

CHAPTER 55

꼭

AFTER THE SPA WENT INTO bankruptcy, I didn't hear from GQ Boy for a couple of months. This surprised me because I was used to him calling me every few days and making some kind of threat, especially with the last one being that he would put me into personal bankruptcy. When he did finally call, there was a moment where my stomach fell to the ground in anticipation of the possibility of losing my home. However, because I've had nothing but time to self-reflect, I was ready to take full responsibility for my actions.

"How are you?" GQ Boy asked politely.

"I'm okay," I lied. "How are you?"

"I'm okay. I wanted to let you know that I paid off the bank loan, so you're off the hook," he said.

"Thank you. I mean it," I replied, softly.

"So what are you going to do now?"

"I don't know. I'm taking some time off right now and trying to figure it out," I paused. "I'm so sorry about everything. I wish I could turn back time and do things differently."

"You know I tried my best," he said.

"I know. I was the one who went and fucked it all up. I'm the stupid idiot," I said. "Thanks again... I mean... for not making me have to move back into my parents' basement."

"Yeah..."

"Can I ask you something?"

"Yes. What is it?"

"Do you hate me? I mean... after all I've done to you?"

"No, I could never hate you. I'll always love you," GQ Boy replied while choking back tears.

"I'll always love you, too. As a dear, dear friend. Can we be friends? I mean, not straightaway because I know the wounds are still fresh, but maybe in time?"

"Yeah, maybe..."

"Well, I'll see you around," I said awkwardly.

"Yeah."

It was the most cordial conversation I'd had with GQ Boy in a long time and it elevated my spirits knowing that he had forgiven me for hurting him. I commend him for his ability to forgive despite all the pain he's been through because if the situation were reverse, I don't know if I would have been able to do the same. His actions captured his true essence of a kind and loving human being showing me that I was not worthy of him because he deserved to be with someone who could love him wholeheartedly. Only time will tell if he'll accept my invitation to remain friends, but in the meantime I know we both need time to heal.

CHAPTER 56

‏ↄϨ‎

AFTER MY MEETING WITH ADE, I went home and pondered for weeks about our conversation and what the correlation was between the spa shutting down and my childhood. I still couldn't connect the two, but I came to the conclusion that if I was chained by my childhood issues, then I needed to release myself from its grip.

When I allowed my tantalizing childhood memories to surface, within minutes I would be consumed with anger and hatred. I would convulse into tears because I didn't have the capacity to propagate changes. I felt in theory the idea was good, but it was rubbish because it couldn't change my past. Therefore, what was the point of conceding to therapy?

"I'm trying to go 'within' like you said, but every time I do, I get so angry. What's the point of all this when the past can't be changed?" I expressed in frustration over the phone one evening.

"It's not about changing the past. It's about understanding yourself, and to do so you must look to the past. As a child you didn't have the proper tools to deal with all the trauma, but now you do. You have no choice... if you don't deal with these feelings now, you will continue to be an angry and hateful individual... and those emotions will always jeopardize any success. Think of this as your death," Ade answered.

"If this is my death, then I want to be reborn into a much stronger and wiser person. I don't want to be the old Lina. I don't want to be consumed with anger and hatred. I want to love myself."

"Well, that's your key. You say you want to love yourself... then figure out what made you start hating yourself in the first place. People aren't born into this world hating themselves. Somewhere along the way, things happened that turned you this way."

"I don't wish my childhood upon my worst enemy. My dad was an abusive alcoholic and my uncle molested me for years while my mom sat back and let it happen!" I screamed in anguish. "I hate them all!"

Ade breathed a long sigh before he said, "You have anger towards your dad for being a drunk, you have hatred toward your uncle for molesting you, and you have resentment towards your mom for not protecting you. The truth is – you are not those emotions," Ade consoled.

"If I'm not all those things, then what am I?" I sobbed. "I'm not a likeable person. Most people think I'm a bitch. I even think so."

"I see someone who's been badly wounded, so she puts up a very harsh exterior to protect herself. The real Lina is a very kind person who is full of love. You asked me why I didn't turn my back on you... because I seek truth and I saw yours all along."

"So you think I'm capable of love?" I sniffled.

"Authentic love is only possible if you love yourself. By loving yourself, all negative thoughts and feelings will be replaced with light and wonderment and you will see the world differently. You will radiate nothing but positivity, and that energy will attract nothing but an abundance of joy into your life," Ade marveled.

"So, all these things about me, like me hating the world and people, and me not believing in love is not really who I am? My whole life, I really thought that that was who I am."

"No, that's not you, Lina. That's scar tissue that you need to get rid of. Underneath the scar tissue is the real Lina. It won't be easy and there will be times when it'll be too much to bare. You basically have to come face-to-face with your deepest fears and demons. Most people don't have the strength or will to take that inward journey. The question is, do you?" Ade challenged.

"I want to take that journey. Like you said... I don't have a choice."

CHAPTER 57

꼭

ACCEPTANCE IS A RELATIVELY EASY term to understand when there's no emotions attached to it. But, if affliction is associated to it, then denial overthrows acceptance.
Denial can occur by deliberately rejecting the existence of the event or by choosing not to think or talk about it. Either way means you're forbidding yourself the
right to recovery.

However, it's always easier to accept things when you understand the nature of the cause. As I knew that I couldn't change the past, my only option
was to accept it. In order to do this, I had to go as far back as to understand my
parents' behavior. Only then could I have true knowledge of why things came
to be and accept my childhood for what it was.

From what Mom told me, she grew up in a small fishing village in an impoverished household where school was considered a luxury. Without the resources
to attend school, Mom grew up to be illiterate. This was the driving force behind her pushing us academically. Education came with greater options and the
pursuit of a better life which was exactly what she wanted for her children. But
sometimes what you want isn't congruent to what you're conditioned to believe.
Her scenario was the cultural ideology that women were second-class citizens
and a man's life would always have more value than a woman's.

Starvation was a daily reality in Mom's family. So from a young age, Mom
had to contribute to the survival of the family which meant working long hours
on the rice fields or selling fish in the local market to earn income. My grandparents were constantly struggling to provide for their nine children, so when
Mom turned eighteen, Grandpa jumped at the opportunity to marry Mom off

when Dad came to ask for her hand in marriage without knowing anything about him.

Dad saw a picture of Mom when he was in jail because his cellmate was dating my aunt. Even though he had never met Mom, that picture was enough for him to know that she was going to be his wife once he got out of jail. A week after his release, he made true on his words and came to Mom's house bearing all sorts of gifts and food. Just like that, my grandpa agreed to marry his prettiest daughter to a complete stranger that had just gotten out of jail. They couldn't have been more mismatched – the short, unattractive city boy with the innocent virgin beauty of the village.

What my grandpa also didn't know was that Dad had a long history of substance abuse stemming from his days fighting in the war alongside the Americans. Most of the soldiers used opium as a way to numb their pain and deal with the horrors that war often evokes. Dad was no different, using opium to cope with the pain of friends dying. He lived with large bullet wounds on his chest and abdomen, a daily reminder that he had survived the war and reinforcing his survival syndrome. After the war, Dad resumed the gangster lifestyle he'd been living since dropping out of school at fifteen, to support his drug use. It was during one of his illegal activities that he wound up in jail. When he married Mom, Dad substituted one addiction with another and used alcohol to comfort himself.

When I evaluate my parents' circumstances, I came to the realization that they too were a direct byproduct of their environment. They were a case where nature and nurture worked harmoniously together to sculpt two flawed individuals who would unconsciously transfer all their pain and agony to their children. Mom couldn't protect me from Uncle Quinn because she was engrained to know a women's place – which was never to question a man's integrity. This explains why she always took Uncle Quinn's words over mine. In the end, the fault always lies within the women because somehow she was responsible for raising a child that was deserving of what her brother did. Her only way to cope was to deny the presence of any molestation. It was all she knew how to do.

However, from the moment Mom chose to silence my voice, her rejection spawned deep resentment and crippled me inside. She made me feel so inadequate. This manifested in me a desire to become an overachiever. I had to prove to her that I was worthy of her love. Yet, the more I achieved, the more I wrestled with feelings of not ever being good enough.

As for Dad, he chose to suppress any feelings pertaining to his time in the war and rarely spoke about it. Drinking made him temporarily forget. However, he inadvertently unleashed his pain in the way of violence towards who he knew was obliged to endure it: Mom. Dad's violent behavior when drunk brought out great fear in me, but worse was the sense of abandonment I felt whenever he would leave me at home alone to go out and drink. His selfish actions left a trail of consequential conduct from me when it came to my relationships with men. I would find myself in a continual string of relationships, for all the wrong reasons, to avoid being alone.

I'm not going to pretend to understand why Uncle Quinn did the things he did to me. Truth be told, I don't care to sympathize with his behavior. His despicable actions decapitated my ability to fully trust men. Therefore, I unwittingly withheld affection from them. Thus, the two most prominent male figures in my life as a child ultimately shattered the image of what a healthy relationship with a male should entail. Instead, I was left in a constant battle of fight or flight.

Thus, I too am a result of my environment. Like my Dad, I suppressed my childhood mishaps into adulthood and released it by way of immense anger towards others and the world. Being consumed by anger automatically generates a great amount of hatred which makes it impossible to love yourself. The emotions of anger and hatred convey so much pain that without forgiveness you're left with self-hatred. If you hate yourself so much like I did, then you're left with the ultimate demise of self-destruction and any success, whether personal or professional, would result in unconscious sabotage.

Going back to look at my parents' history, I was able to address my own issues. I was finally able to see what Ade had been trying to tell me all along: "The spa shutting down was no coincidence. This was bound to happen. It had nothing to do with you, GQ Boy, or little buddy there. Any unresolved emotional issues from your past need to be dealt with or else this will continue to happen again. The next time you build something, it will collapse. The only difference is the people in the story will be different."

CHAPTER 58

྾

I FEEL LIKE FORGIVENESS IS always something easier said than done. When you've held onto anger for as long as I have, letting it go seems daunting. If it's all you've known the majority of your life, the promise of joy, and happiness on the other side makes me contemplate whether it's as good as it's cracked out to be. That's the grisly part of transformation. In order to transform you must strip away old habits, thoughts and feelings and this doesn't happen overnight; rather, it's a slow arduous process.

Forgiveness is a journey in itself. It needs to manifest organically in order to authenticate the experience. It's not as simple as accepting an apology from those who have wronged you because if this were true, why do so many of us recant the past, bringing that person's wrongful actions up every time there's an argument? True forgiveness can only happen when you relinquish that person's power over you, claim it for yourself and not allowing the name of that person to trigger any emotion from you. That's why forgiveness *is* the process. You can't strategize on how to forgive because that's like claiming to know the exact moment when that person no longer has any effect on you. One cannot simply plan that.

With Mom, the sentiment I held against her was that of resentment. I need-ed to free myself from it because I realized that resentment was the main cul-prit in why my relationship with her has always been tumultuous and I wanted nothing more than to feel love for her. My intentions were to talk to her calmly about that fateful afternoon as we never spoke of it. However, when I brought it up, my inner child—the one that had been silenced all these years—unleashed a seismic wave of anger, making sure that my voice would be heard this time around.

"Why didn't you believe me when I ran downstairs after he molested me and told you? Why?" I asked screaming.

"I didn't know," Mom denied. "You were so young. Are you sure you remembered correctly?"

"That's exactly why I know it's true because I was so young. I can remember it like it was yesterday!" I said. "You know after all these years you still won't take responsibility for your own actions. You still won't admit any wrongdoing. You didn't believe it then and you still don't believe me now."

"I'm sorry… it was just so long ago and now you're bringing it up out of the blue. I don't know what to think," Mom replied.

"That's fine. You can deny this whole thing ever happened, but next time you wonder why our relationship is always strained, you'll know why," I told her.

"Please don't be like this," Mom begged.

"Be like what? Mom, I want so badly to forgive you. I want to move on with my life. But I find it so hard to do when you won't acknowledge that your brother molested me. It's clear that you chose him over me years ago and you still continue to do so," I said.

"What do you mean? I'm not choosing him over you. You're my daughter."

"You still have a relationship with him!" I yelled.

"He's my brother. You can't expect me to cut him out of my life," Mom said defensively.

"No, I can't. But what I can do is cut you out of my life," I bawled as I hung up the phone, wondering for the millionth time why my mother doesn't love me.

"I've been trying to call you for weeks," Mom said. "I wanted to apologize but you wouldn't take my calls. I want you to know that I'm sorry I didn't believe you then, but I believe you now. I'm sorry I didn't protect you from him. I'm cutting him out of my life and disowning him. He'll no longer be a part of this family. I should have done that a long time ago."

Sometimes forgiveness is a two-way street. The other person needs time to reflect on their actions and come to terms with it. In the Asian culture, a parent never apologizes to their child even when they are blatantly wrong. Your parents are considered your elders and therefore more superior. To have Mom break tradition and apologize to me finally gave me the validation that I'd been longing for my whole life from her. I finally knew that she does love me and I do matter to her.

Even though I wholeheartedly accepted her apology, it was only the beginning of my recovery process. I still wasn't in the space where my resentment towards her was fully renounced. There were times where her presence was welcomed with ease and other times old feelings would creep out. I would fell pangs of discomfort, but so long as my journey towards transformation was marked with more progression than regression, our situation was still a milestone to celebrate.

While I hated the fact that Dad's addiction brought so much turmoil to our family, it was fairly easy for me to forgive him. In his later years, when he was diagnosed with liver cirrhosis, he stopped drinking and became the loving and gentle husband Mom always wished for. Dad possessed a quiet stillness while reflecting on his life and I immediately recognized a transformation happening to him alongside my own. I felt so much empathy towards Dad. And witnessing his transformation, even though it came later in his life, proved to me his level of awareness and that was enough for me to fully forgive him. The fear I used to feel around him was replaced by warm thoughts and a profound love that brought us closeness. As for any feelings of abandonment, sometimes the ability to gauge where the problem stems from is all you need in order to move on and change past behaviors.

Perhaps the hardest person for me to forgive was Uncle Quinn. I hadn't seen him since I was a teenager, when he moved away to another province. News that he had moved back after all these years brought upon a rising tension in me, holding me emotionally hostage, even though physically he couldn't hurt me anymore. He was someone I didn't care to ever see or speak to again in my life, so confronting him about his past actions was not an option. Regardless of how many times I told myself to selflessly forgive him so that I could be free, it all fell flat because I couldn't. Just the thought of him brought about so much hatred in me that I was unsure if I could ever get past it.

But as I mentioned, forgiveness is a journey that can't be planned and so one evening I found myself eating at a restaurant and in walked Uncle Quinn. Immediately, I froze in terror. My heart palpitated with immense anxiety. I was brought back to my six-year-old self where I felt helpless and defenseless. My immediate reaction was to get out of that restaurant but somehow I forced myself to stay long enough to finish my meal. From where he was sitting, I knew he couldn't see me, so I sat and studied him. He had aged quite a bit and his wrinkles showed the strain of his divorce drama as well as a life lived in solitude with no friends, evidenced by him dining by himself. After watching him for a while and feeling his lonesome energy, I saw a weak and pathetic individual. In that moment, a quiet voice within me whispered, "I forgive you." And I slipped away unnoticed by him.

CHAPTER 59

ơ♭

PART OF LOVING YOURSELF IS facing challenging decisions that you don't want to make. In my case, the toughest thing I had to do, more than losing the spa, was breaking up with Aiden. After the spa shut down, our differences seemed to surface overnight, making for a turbulent relationship. The red flags were there from the beginning, but I chose to ignore them because, like Ade said, I was in love with the image of love and not the actuality.

The reality was that from day one we were both at different points in our lives and the commonality that united us was what Aiden symbolized: young love. Aiden replaced what should have been with Miguel, reflecting the nature of where I was emotionally – that of a stunted teenager. Therefore, the gap between our ages was bridged and made us emotionally equivalent. I mistakenly interpreted our heated passion as love, when the reality was that it was nothing more than infatuation. Despite what people say about love being hard work, I like to think that it shouldn't be. Love, when with the right person, should be effortless and easy.

I now know that the energy you put out in the universe is also the same energy that you'll attract in your life. This couldn't be truer of Aiden and me. We both portrayed the best image to each other initially, but as the years passed, I would learn that Aiden was a lost and angry soul trying his best in all his capabilities to figure himself out… which was exactly where I was. The difference was how we approached our issues. Aiden turned to excessive partying, involving heavy drinking and drug use. I chose to self-medicate in a healthy, holistic lifestyle that involved the usage of an herbal, plant-based diet.

Even though our paths were polar opposites, I still spent most of our time together trying to get him to change. I felt like I had sacrificed everything to be with him, so in return he owed it to me to work harder. On Aiden's behalf, I believe I was an easy convenience in his life and only a part of his journey in that moment in time. In addition, I felt like Aiden never really got over my escorting past, so there was a lot of respect lost towards me. Even though it was something he never admitted to, it was a presence I always felt.

Our once-intense obsession with one another was replaced with furious fights that brought out the worst in me with my incessant neediness and smothering ways. In my mind, my love for Aiden was very real and I was petrified to lose him. I couldn't possibly live without him. A life without Aiden meant that I would have to face my ultimate fear of being alone. I wasn't ready to do that so I would make up excuses for Aiden, mainly that he was young and just needed time to mature and grow into that perfect man for me.

Eventually, I learned to accept that time doesn't change anything; rather, actions change things. I had run out of excuses for Aiden. And I knew that part of truly loving myself was to leave the one person that I believed I loved so dearly. I had to prove to myself that I loved myself more, and that I deserved to be happy with someone all the time and not just sometimes.

The breakup happened on a Sunday when the stark reality that I was never going to be a priority in Aiden's life, despite how much I cared for him, sunk into my chest.

"Hey Aiden, I was wondering if you can pick up that coat I had my eye on when we were at the mall last week? I'll give you the money for it," I asked while getting ready for work.

"I don't know. We'll see," Aiden replied. I could tell he felt lousy because of his hangover from his previous night's partying.

"What do you mean? Did you have other plans for today?" I asked.

"No. I just don't feel like going to the mall on my day off," he replied.

Asshole.

"Can't you just do me this one favor? I would go myself but I don't have time and it would mean a lot to me," I told him.

"Okay!" he replied.

"Thanks," I said.

However, that evening when I returned home from work, there was no coat to be found. Instead, a lazy Aiden was sprawled across my couch.

"Did you pick up that coat?" I asked.

"No."

"What do you mean? Did something happen?" I questioned.

"No. I was just really hungry, so I went to get something to eat instead," Aiden replied.

"And you couldn't go to the mall afterwards? It would have taken all but fifteen minutes out of your day," I replied.

"Look... I just didn't want to, okay?" he replied.

Tears began rolling down my face.

"I have spent the last four years of my life being the best girlfriend to you," I said. "I cook, clean and do everything you ask of me. How many times have I picked you up in the middle of the night when you're out partying and can't find a taxi home? How many times have I driven you to your car the following morning? I never complain and, in fact, I do it happily because I love you. Now I ask you for a simple favor and you can't even return it."

"What's the big deal? So I didn't pick up a coat for you today. You can pick it up yourself tomorrow," he responded.

"If you can't even do such a simple thing for me, then what's the point of being together?" I bawled. "I want to break up."

"You're breaking up with me because I didn't pick up a coat for you?" he asked.

"It's not about the coat... it's what it signifies. If you don't love me enough to pick up a damn coat, then I know you'll be the first one out the door when we have real problems!" I yelled.

"Well, I stuck by you with the whole spa mess, didn't I?" he hollered back.

"Only because you had nothing to lose. I gave up everything to be with you and after all this time together you still can't fully commit to me."

"What do you mean? I am committed."

"You refuse to move in together. You only drop by my place when it's convenient for you and you need me to nurse your hangover. I'm not looking to take care of a child. I'm looking for a partner… someone who has my back and who loves me enough to pick up a fuckin' coat for me on his day off when he's got nothing to do! Get out of my house and get out of my life!" I screamed.

Within minutes of breaking up, I walked around my apartment to gather all of Aiden's belongings for him while he stood reactionless by the front door. I think deep down inside he was truly relieved of the great favor I was bestowing upon him. The only thing he cared to take was his bottle of Johnny Walker.

As one last nice gesture, I even offered to drop off his dry cleaning the following day and leave it on his doorstep.

"Well, make sure it's after 4:00 when I get off work," he said. "I don't want it sitting outside to get stolen by someone if I'm not home."

I thought he might have cared enough to muster words of kindness during our breakup. But what he said proved how self-centered he was and that I did deserve much better. I could have told him to go fuck himself; instead, I necessitated his request so that I couldn't dispute with myself that I did everything in my power to make the relationship work.

"So this is it?" Aiden asked after sitting in my car silently for five minutes.

"Yes, this is it," I replied. I watched Aiden walk away with such emptiness, knowing that this was the last time I would ever see him. It would be too hard for me to remain friends with him. As a woman, there's nothing worse than knowing that the person you loved never loved you back.

In the weeks that followed, Aiden didn't bother calling me to see how I was doing. This came as no shock to me. After the spa shut down, I was always the one chasing him and fighting for the relationship. Initially I handled the breakup quite well, feeling more anger towards him than anything, but when the reality of our breakup finally permeated, I realized that there would be no getting back together like the many other times. I grieved it like a death. I spent days unable to get out of bed. In my weakest moments, when the pain was too ferocious to handle, I convinced myself that I was better off in an unhappy relationship than to endure this pain.

When I finally succumbed to the pain and called Aiden, he drove the stake deeper into my heart by telling me that he had moved on and had no interest in getting back together. In hindsight, it was a blessing in disguise, but when you're in the midst of the storm it never feels like that. It took many lonely nights reading the works of Lao Tzu, Osho, and Krishnamurti—just to name a few—to propel me out my abyss and finally face what I'd been avoiding my whole life: my fear of being alone.

When you face your fears head-on, it's true what those books say: "The feelings of fear, anxiety, nostalgia, and discomfort will all eventually disappear because they have nowhere left to go." What remained were the chantings of my inner voice, repeating for me to love myself and that I was worthy of love.

Reading those self-help books helped me compartmentalize many things. One of them was that we are one hundred percent accountable for our own happiness. We can't rely on anyone to make us happy. I was always dependent on someone or something to make me feel happy – whether it was a relationship or material things. When I finally took responsibility for the failures of my past relationships, instead of blaming it on the other person, I was able to see my life so clearly. I finally grasped what Ade had been telling me all this time: "When you see, you can't unsee." Somehow, let the notion of controlling all things dissipate because, in the end, the only security we have is insecurity.

CHAPTER 60

∞

FORGIVING THOSE WHO HAVE HURT you is critical to your healing process. But another aspect of healing that is quite often overlooked is, apologizing to those you've hurt. The one person deserving of an apology from me was GQ Boy. My apologies to GQ Boy during the spa days were nothing more than empty vocals. The apologies were understated due to my narcissistic ways, hence in hindsight it never came from the right place.

The old saying, "When you know better, you do better" is so fitting because with much spiritual growth, I felt strong about expressing my gratitude towards him. I decided to write a letter because there's something endearing about writing your thoughts on paper rather than speaking it. The purpose of the letter wasn't to stir up old emotions, but to articulate how much I appreciated his friendship. Given the history that Aiden, he and I shared, he became an unlikely source to help me through my heartache with Aiden. However, he was there whenever I needed some comfort.

I needed him to know that through self-actualization and much clarity, I've recognized why I behaved the way I did. Only now did I feel in my heart that I was able to give him a sincere apology and convey the depths of regret I have for my actions that caused him much pain.

If there's one important thing I've learned through my journey, it's that anyone, regardless of their socioeconomic standing, needs to feel appreciated and validated. The mere fact that GQ Boy chose to forgive me long ago and maintain a friendship with me, despite all that I'd done, speaks volumes about the kind of person he is – a kind, generous and loving person.

It took me a while to pen the letter because I wanted to be cognizant of my words. When I was finally done, I felt much satisfaction.

"Read it when you get home," I told him as I handed him the letter one evening after dinner.

Weeks later, when we met up again and I asked if he had read the letter, I received a smile in return. His smile was so perfect in its simplicity; it was enough for me to know that he understood. Since then, we've never had to speak of our past again. Afterwards, I came home feeling so light inside and blessed to have such a wonderful person in my life.

It's funny how life turns out sometimes. I always thought that Aiden was the one who would always be a part of my life, not GQ Boy. But I wouldn't have it any other way. Relationships, whether platonic or romantic, need to add value to your life in order for you to invest your time into growing and nurturing it. My relationship with GQ Boy encompassed all that, and he has also evolved throughout the years. What started out as strictly business grew into romance and ended in the best possible way – friendship.

CHAPTER 61

॰ৡ৽

AFTER INSTIGATING FORGIVENESS AND APOLOGY, I spent several years committed to different teachings and works that would elevate me spiritually. I wanted to live in a continual state of love and acceptance towards myself. But the truth was that wasn't always happening. There would be times when I'd feel more in touch with myself and other times the hectic day-to-day noise of the outside world would clog my path preventing me from feeling at ease. Like any clogged pipe, eventually it will burst and when it did, I would find remnants of my former self escaping by way of self-hatred. Eventually that led to a setback where I went through a period that I couldn't make any sense of, though my intuition was strongly telling me that what I was feeling was the last leg of my transformation. If I could figure out what this resurfaced turmoil was and do the work to release it, then I will be free of any past contentions and finally be able to love myself wholly.

I needed to shed my last ten pounds of emotional weight. I like to compare the process to that of losing physical weight. We all know that the first twenty or thirty pounds are the easiest to lose. But it's the last ten pounds that are the most challenging. It's that last bit that's ridiculously stubborn and will hang on for dear life. Unless you're willing to dig deep and push yourself to the next level, that last ten pounds will continue to store itself in you.

Emotional weight is very much the same because our bodies are comprised of trillions of cells that consume space. Each of these cells stores some form of emotional weight. And whether you believe it or not, how can one explain the perception of feeling much lighter when you release yourself of the emotional burdens that you've carried around your whole life? Because our emotional stresses do have weight to them and, like physical weight, the last ten pounds *is the hardest to shed!*

With Ade's urging, I enlisted the help of a Reiki master to help channel positive energy and clear out the negative, in hopes that I would feel more balanced. However, through the course of several weeks, the Reiki master applied guided meditation into our sessions. This cleared any blockages and shed much light onto what was hindering me from moving forward.

Guided meditation is exactly as it sounds. During this process, the Reiki master helps facilitate you into a Zen state by ways of soothing words or with a combination of energy work. In that tranquil space, your mind is free to explore whatever thoughts, feelings, or emotions it desires. Every guided meditation has a different outcome, with some ending in nothing more than your body feeling rested while others take you further inside to probe for answers that only your subconscious knows.

Almost immediately, I was fortunate enough to benefit from guided meditation. And, by our third session, a breakthrough happened. Our session started off with my Reiki master chanting calming words and asking me to focus on my breath. Before long I found myself in what seemed like a dream... but a dream that I was fully aware of.

I see a little girl with long black hair and bangs standing naked in front of me. Instinctively, I know that this is my six-year-old self. I embrace her in my arms.

"It wasn't your fault," I tell her. "There was nothing you could have done differently. You'll grow up to be okay. We grew up to be okay. I love you and you'll always be a part of me."

Suddenly, my six-year-old self morphs into my three-year-old self. She's a toddler with short hair, a protruding belly, pudgy fingers and she's wearing a yellow t-shirt with blue jeans. She looks up at me with big brown eyes and smiles. I hug her tenderly as I ask her to step inside a nearby canoe. We make our way up the river where we stop at an island. In the distance, I hear the laughter of many children, and even though I can't see them, I know they're playing and having a wonderful time.

"You'll be safe here," I say. "Everything will okay. I'll always be with you."

I proceed up the river in the canoe. I see a woman holding a baby. I can't make out who's carrying the baby because I only see her back. But, I see the baby very clearly and it is my six-month-old self. The baby has a head full of hair and a bright smile on her face.

"You're so beautiful and innocent. How can anyone ever hurt you?" I ask in awe.

What felt like five minutes was in reality fifty minutes because that's what mediation does. In meditation, there is no concept of time. What I took away from that experience was that I needed to say goodbye to my inner child in order to move on.

My six-year-old self represented the beginning of the sexual abuse. Her standing naked was a metaphor of how she was violated. The three-year-old portrayed the abandonment I felt from my dad. Dropping her off at the island full of other children meant that she would never be alone. My six-month old self is symbolic of the innocence we are all brought into this world with.

There's a reason as to why I saw myself from oldest to youngest. It's like peeling back the layers of an onion. You have to peel the outer layer first, your most recent memories, in order to reach the core where truth and beauty lie. The closer you get to the core of the onion is where you'll feel the largest degree of discomfort from the enzymes that are released that burn your eyes – the difficulty of shedding the last ten pounds. However, when the hard part is over, you'll find that there is nothing purer than the innocence of a baby. Finally, you'll be able to see the world unfiltered just like one.

The Reiki master also introduced emotional transmutation into our session that brought attention to something I never even knew I carried. Emotional transmutation comes back to what I previously mentioned about our cells carrying emotional weight. Through this process, my Reiki master was able to take a very specific emotion and parlay that back to the initial event that made us feel that emotion. The point of going back to that first moment is to acknowledge its existence and then to release it from us, just like going back to the original source in order to destroy it.

After the materialization of my inner child, I started reading about the meaning behind your inner child emerging. Through my research, I had an epiphany: I realized that I had been carrying around the feeling of shame my entire life. This underlying emotion was stronger than the fear, abandonment, and resentment I possessed.

Shame is much like a chameleon. It hides itself very well in other emotions; hence, the reason why I never felt shame in my daily life. My projecting perfectionism in all that I do and deviation towards material wealth was an attempt to be validated. This, and the self-jeopardizing of my personal relationships are *all* outcomes of feeling shame.

Initially, I was under the impression that the shame was born from being molested. Even though I've acknowledged that it was not my fault, sex was always something that made me feel so dirty. The whole time I was an escort, I felt disgusted with myself and the reason I was so successful at it was because I was able to channel my own self-hatred into a powerful tool to suppress the shame.

Shame is also the main culprit in why I could never fully be intimate in a relationship because it didn't allow me to be. Let's not confuse the act of sex with intimacy. They are two completely different things. Sex is an act or action while intimacy deals with connectivity, the ability for two people to simultaneously engage in emotional bondage. The closest I've come to experiencing intimacy was with Aiden. But, my speculation that he still cast judgment on my sexual past was the sneaky shame that was hidden in me, therefore halting me from ever being intimate with him at a full capacity.

Upon the discovery that shame was the primal reason that inhibited me from moving forward, I asked my Reiki master to use emotional transmutation to bring me back to that day where I was six... the day that Uncle Quinn violently and sexually abused me. I was warned ahead of time that this would be the most intense session of all as it was addressing the root of all – my emotional trauma. But, I was ready for it.

As I was guided through by the tranquil voice of my Reiki master, she openly summoned the shame. I entered into meditation where very much like before,

I was dreaming with full alertness. I see my five-year-old self in red pants and a baseball-style t-shirt, where the sleeves are red and the rest of the shirt is white with a rainbow spread across the front. I have on pink Velcro sneakers and I can remember that this was my favorite outfit. I'm looking up at Mom and she's a very young thirty-year-old that's dressed in her Sunday best and looking absolutely stunning. She's pointing her index finger at me and yelling while I'm staring back at her – my sweet innocent face doesn't have a clue as to why she's so upset with me. Suddenly, my present self starts crying profusely and my Reiki master instructs me to tell Mom how I feel.

"Mom, stop yelling at me. What did I do?" I ask mentally, but I get no answer from Mom.

As the tears continue to flow, my Reiki master pulls me back to the present. She abruptly stops the session and I am left feeling absolutely drained. I am shocked by the outcome. I came into emotional transmutation certain that it was the sexual abuse that initiated my feelings of shame. I was finally able to understand that by Mom yelling at me after Uncle Quinn abused me, it reignited the shame and linked it to the sexual abuse. However, the initial moment of shame happened when I was five.

The first seven years of a child's life is the most important in terms of creating the foundation for psychological development. Unfortunately, all the emotions that I developed before the age of seven were all negative based on the way I was raised. If our cells hold emotional memory, then I know that Mom's is no different. To release my shame incidentally means to release Mom from hers, because I am her. I come from her cells. Through awareness, I was finally able to absolve Mom from my emotional burdens and this revelation was the catapult I needed to shed my last ten pounds.

CHAPTER 62

PERHAPS THE LAST PERSON I needed to forgive in order to truly move on was me. I wish forgiving myself was as simple as saying, "I forgive you. Now go and love yourself." But it's not. Forgiving oneself is a progression through self-actualization that could take many years to manifest.

In my scenario, I was the last person on my list to be forgiven. I had to go through deep reflection with everyone else first in order to understand myself. Once I understood, I was able to release myself from any burdens and see that my prior actions towards others and myself came from a pain-ridden self rather than my authentic self. To honor my authentic self, I had to start living my life ultimately differently than before instead of falling back into the same inner trappings. That meant living each day with full consciousness that everything you put out into the universe will determine what you get back.

Instead of falling into my old pattern of jumping into another relationship after my breakup from Aiden, I decided to be in a relationship with myself and rediscover what it was that I really liked. Too often, we get into relationships and are influenced by what our partner's interests are, only to realize afterwards that those weren't even ours to begin with. Being in a relationship with yourself means that your number one priority is yourself. I was determined to treat myself well just like I would any other partner. That started with me appreciating my body for everything that it does for me. In turn, I replaced all negative thoughts with positive ones, filling me up with gratitude.

With gratitude I was able to accept grace into my life and through grace, I found myself for the first time truly liking people and opening myself up into trusting others. I was able to make the connection that life was all about relationships, not about money, and so I started building new friendships.

Eventually, the hatred inside of me started filling up with love. And, one morning I woke up feeling nothing but an overwhelming acceptance: *I AM ENOUGH.* I would no longer need approval from anybody else to validate my own self-worth. I am all there needs to be. In knowing that, I realized that love is not complicated. Rather, it is so transparent because unconditional love has no strings attached and casts no judgment.

My whole life, I felt like I was always standing in the shadows of darkness. Now, I was standing underneath a golden arch that radiated so brightly. All strains of shame were replaced by an unadulterated love and for the first time ever, I was in love with life!

When I was ready for love again, I met Marcus. I'd seen him many times at the gym and it so happened that we had a mutual friend that ended up introducing us. On our first date, we decided to meet at a lounge and when I walked in I found Marcus in the back holding a fresh bouquet of flowers.

"Hi," Marcus said hugging me. "These are for you."

Wow! It's been a long time since I've gotten flowers.

"Thank you!" I beamed, as I checked out his tall lean frame.

"Can I take your coat for you?" he asked.

Such a gentleman. I love it!

"Yes, thank you," I replied. "So Marcus, tell me a little bit about yourself."

"Well, I'm originally from Latvia. I've been in Canada for two years now on a work permit."

I made a mental note that he had a sexy European accent.

"How do you like it here?" I asked, admitting his sharp facial features that blended into a ménage of perfection.

"It's different but I like it. There's more opportunities here than back home."

"What do you do for work right now?"

"For now, I work in construction but eventually I'd like to own my own business of some kind," Marcus answered.

"So you're ambitious," I remarked.

"Well, I just don't want to waste any opportunities I get here. I find people here take things for granted and they like to complain."

"I couldn't agree more," I laughed. "What do you like to do on your days off?"

"I rarely get any time off work. Right now I'm working seven days a week."

"Wow, that's a lot. So no time for partying," I joked.

"No, I partied enough in Europe. My partying days are over. It's all about work for me now."

"I like how you think. It's very much an immigrant mentality where you work hard and not take anything for granted."

"I wouldn't take you for granted," Marcus blushed. "I mean if we were together."

Wow, he's smooth. I like him.

As we effortlessly chatted well into the night, I was certain I wanted to see him again until he stunned me with his age... ten years my junior.

"Well, age is just a number right?" Marcus said smiling.

"Yeah... sure," I replied hesitantly.

How can this be? He looks so much older and is so mature.

After I got over the shock of his age, I spent days deliberating over whether or not I wanted to see him again. There were so many things that I liked about him aside from the obvious physical attraction. I liked that we had very similar values and work ethics derived from our immigrant background. And I appreciated his chivalry because I was certain that chivalry had become obsolete in the younger generation. However, I was insistent on not repeating the same mistakes I had with Aiden. And with Marcus being so close in age with Aiden, it made me question myself harder.

Why am I attracted to yet another younger guy? Is this representative of me not moving past the emotional maturity of a teenage girl? Is this some kind of setback... a regression of sorts?

Then I discerned that I was already taking a snapshot of what I thought Marcus might be like. Logistically I was forecasting what a relationship with him would entail based on my previous experience with Aiden. If I were a different person, which I knew that I was, then I had to forge a clean slate. I couldn't condemn myself to a foreseeable future that has not even existed based on my prior actions. Doing that would mean that I have not evolved. It's no different than playing the same CD repeatedly and expecting a different song at the end.

If I was all that I needed, then being in a relationship with a partner is an added bonus, only to enhance my existing love for my life and myself. There was no need to contemplate because contemplation equals expectations and expectations are what lead to the collapse of all relationships.

The relationship has to come with no expectations. Expectations go back to taking that snapshot of what you want it to be versus what it really is, which is something organic that you have to allow to develop naturally. Only in that freedom are you truly able to enjoy the relationship for what it is.

By no means does this depth reflect a pattern of falling for the same type. Rather, it's a keen sense of awareness that when you judge someone, you mistakenly judge yourself. I was done with judging myself, so I trudged forward with no trepidation and allowed myself to be.

From the beginning, there was no ego to be found in our relationship. We were able to immerse ourselves in a drama-free environment that provided much support and growth towards each other's personal development. We fully understood that we were two people fortunate enough to walk alongside each other down this path called life.

Being together doesn't mean we possess ownership of the relationship because at any given time, either one of us is free to leave. We are together, knowing that it's because we want to be and not because we have to be, essentially making fights between us few and far between because we are not bound by one another. We are only bound by the impermanence that, just as our body will one day return to its original source of nothing, so too will this relationship. In this sentiment, it's important to appreciate the relationship for all that it is and not take anything for granted.

Marcus expressed on our first date that he doesn't take things for granted. This set the premise for our relationship in terms of us appreciating the way we both elevate each other. This relationship is by far the healthiest and easiest relationship I've ever been in. I mentioned that relationships shouldn't be hard;

rather, with the right person, they should be effortless. With Marcus, it was. Somewhere in that first year, I gave my heart over completely to him and, soon after, Marcus and I were living together.

One early morning, Marcus tapped me on my shoulder waking me up.

"What is it?" I yawned.

"Will you marry me?" Marcus asked, pulling out a beautiful princess cut diamond ring.

"Are you serious?" I asked.

"Yes."

"No, you can't be." I said.

"I am," Marcus replied. "So... will you?"

"Yes," I laughed. "Of course!"

When you love yourself, you radiate and attract nothing but the purest love into your life.

CHAPTER 63

SHORTLY AFTER OUR ENGAGEMENT, MY family was dealt a huge blow when Dad's health took a turn for the worse. Dad, like most men, avoided going to the doctor. He was forced to go when seemingly overnight his entire body had swelled up and his skin tone was a distinct yellow. This heightened our suspicion that it had something to do with his liver cirrhosis. Carmen diligently took Dad to all of his doctor's appointments. But, it was me who took him to the most daunting one of all, the test results.

As we sat in the oncologist's office waiting for the doctor, Dad turned to me with worrisome eyes and asked, "Do you think I'll be okay?"

"Yes, Dad. You'll be fine. Let's just wait for the doctor and see what he has to say," I responded reassuringly.

The truth was, I didn't need a doctor to tell me that my dad was dying. I already felt it in my heart. If you're conscious of life, then you're also conscious of death. Both are one and the same. To live is to die and to die is to live. Just as the birth of new life comes with a sweet scent, death also has a distinct smell associated to it. Sitting closely to Dad, I can smell pungent disintegrating flesh.

"I'm sorry to tell you that your dad has stage four liver cancer. He's got a ten-centimeter mass on his liver and numerous ones that measure around one centimeter. There's nothing we can do for him because it's progressed too far. At this time our best option is to send him home and keep him as comfortable as possible," the doctor told us.

"How much time does he have?" I asked.

"Less than a year... I'd say just months."

I closed my eyes and fought back tears as the doctor left the room, hating that I was the one to break the news to Dad.

"Dad," I whispered softly. "You've got liver cancer. There's nothing they can do... it's only a matter of months."

"It's okay. There's no need to feel sad. Let's go home," Dad replied calmly.

The days leading up to Dad's death were heart wrenching. Dad had whittled down to a shadow of his former self. The larger-than-life father I once knew who was full of energy and bold laughter was now replaced by a very quiet person awaiting his mortality.

You learn the most about someone when they're dying. In the last months of Dad's life, I learnt that he was a courageous man who risked his life for the family that he loved to bring us to Canada.

His addictions and faults highlighted that he was human and made mistakes like the rest of us. The great part was that he was able to come to terms with his past and in his last few words expressed that he lived with no regrets and he'll die a proud and dignified man from the wonderful family he leaves behind.

Dad passed away at the hospital early one morning exactly four months after he was diagnosed. The only person in the room with Dad was Carmen, which initially upset me because I wasn't the one beside him in his last moments. But there's beautiful symbolism to that because Dad was the first person Carmen saw when she entered this world. And Carmen was the last person Dad saw as he was leaving, making life come full circle.

What I learned from Dad's passing is that the relationship you have with the first man in your life, your father, is the most important. It sets up the premise of how you view yourself. Even though Dad and I got off to a bumpy start, I was so grateful that I was able to move past the pain he brought upon my family. And, I filled up the remainder of his last few years with such fond memories.

CHAPTER 64

$\wp$

DAD'S DEATH MADE ME REALLY question for the first time whether or not I wanted to have children. I've watched for many years my friends start families. It was something I always procrastinated because being a mother was something I never yearned for. One could argue that it's a result of my childhood circumstances but it wasn't. I knew the level of consciousness required to raise a proper human being and I wasn't sure if I had the capacity to do that. I felt like I didn't have enough to teach my offspring because I was still a student learning the ways of life. Until the student becomes the master, then what is the point of bringing a child into this world, only for it to live unconsciously?

I feel that Dad was telling me from above that I was ready for motherhood when he chose to do it by way of a dog named Bobo. Originally, Bobo was bought for Mom because she was so lonely after Dad's death. The idea was that a dog would keep her company. However, Mom never owned a pet before and didn't know how to handle an eight-week-old puppy. So after two weeks, she pawned him off on me. Initially, I didn't want Bobo because I felt like I was in no position to give this puppy the attention it required. But Marcus was keen on keeping him. It wasn't that I didn't like Bobo—he was the cutest Shih-Tzu ever—it's just that I didn't want to put in the time.

I reluctantly agreed after much persuasion from Marcus. And once I committed to keeping Bobo, I connected immediately with him. Just when I thought I couldn't possibly love anymore, I loved Bobo even more.

It was a whole new kind of love pouring out of me – a profound joy to have him in my life. Regardless of how many pairs of shoes he'd chew or how many accidents he would have in the house, I still loved him.

The way I interacted with Bobo took everyone by surprise because I used to be terrified of dogs. Carmen had been attacked by a small dog when we were kids. I bared witness to it, leaving me traumatized into my adult years. Incidentally, it was only when I started my transformation journey that my fear of dogs subsided, proving that there is nothing but love once you get over fear.

I think we all have much to learn from dogs. From what I observe, dogs are born with their hearts unlocked, revealing their natural state of being which is love. A puppy is born with no awareness and learns through training and reinforcement by its owner. If it's hurt by its owner, it's able to easily forgive and continue on living in the present moment, epitomizing what it is to love unconditionally. Dogs are in tune with all energy and emotions surrounding them, resulting in an ego-less presence, merely existing for your abiding love.

In contrast, humans are born with their hearts locked and part of the human journey is to find keys along the way to unlock your heart. If we manage to unlock our heart by the time our journey ends, then according to Buddhist philosophies, we have reached enlightenment. One could argue that the innocence of a newborn baby is pure. This may be true, but the minute the baby's brain starts developing, the message conveyed by its parents is not to trust. By the time the child is conscious, the heart is already locked. Like a dog, a human's natural state of being is love, but unfortunately we go through life with so many filters that humanity's fullest potential will never be known.

Bobo was a key that unlocked a dormant part of my heart. I can only assume that that's what motherhood feels like. Having children is a key that unlocks part of the human heart. It reveals the endless amount of love you can have towards another person. People always say Bobo is so lucky to have me. But I like to say that I am the lucky one, because in him, I realize that I absolutely have the ability to nurture another human being.

EPILOGUE

꼭

YEARS AGO, I WENT TO an energy reader who told me I was on a spiritual journey that would result in a major transformation. She continued by telling me that there was a place that was calling me; however, she couldn't quite place the location. If I went home and turned on my TV, it would reveal the location. I thought it was a little bizarre and didn't know what to make of it. But when I got home and turned on my TV, the very first image I saw was that of Machu Picchu. My mouth dropped in disbelief, knowing full-well this wasn't a coincidence. The TV could have been showing a million other things. But it had to be a documentary on Machu Picchu, one of the most spiritual places on Earth.

After that discovery, I was on a quest to get myself to Machu Picchu. When it finally came time to plan the trip, I knew that I wanted to hike up to Machu Picchu instead of taking the modern-day train that gets you there in one day. It was important for me to feel the energy of the surrounding nature and become a part of it. I wanted to experience the journey in getting to the destination rather than just the destination itself. This was an adventure I was ready to embark on my own, but Marcus was adamant about joining me to ensure my safety and I welcomed him.

The hike was four days involving an alternative route to Machu Picchu versus the traditional Inca trail, which was my first choice but was unfortunately full. I was warned ahead of time about the high altitude but I overlooked the chances of getting altitude sickness because both Marcus and I were in good shape. The three days we spent in the nearby city of Cusco to acclimatize, failed to rattle up any symptoms, so we neglected to take any medication. However, upon leaving Cusco and commencing on our hike, I fell victim to the altitude almost immediately. There were nine of us in total on our hiking group including our guide, and everyone was all right except for me.

I was ignorant to the detrimental symptoms of altitude sickness. I wasn't aware of what it entailed and being an avid hiker, I was cocky in believing that I was immune to it. Within the first half hour of our hike, I experienced great shortness of breath and had a tremendously difficult time keeping up with the rest of the group. Eventually, I fell behind and spent the majority of the hike alone with Marcus and our guide checking in on me every so often.

The air gets thinner the higher the altitude, so every breath I was inhaling wasn't getting me enough oxygen. As a result, every pound you carry on your back feels like ten, eventually to the point where Marcus had to carry my backpack for me along with his own. Luckily, Marcus wasn't affected by the altitude; instead, he felt more energetic than ever which baffled our entire group. The hike was something I would normally find to be fairly easy. But because of my altitude sickness it was ridiculously hard. Very often, I would have to stop for breaks, making me double-guess myself as to why I signed up for this hike.

When nighttime fell and I couldn't remove my collapsed body amongst the rocks, I was aided by a donkey who carried me to camp. As I cocooned myself in my sleeping bag, trying to stay warm from the freezing evening temperature, I wondered, *Does it have to be this unbearable? Does it have to be so damn cold? Couldn't I understand the meaning of all this without feeling so miserable?*

As our hike progressed to the highest summit point of 4,750 meters above sea level, my condition worsened. I could no longer physically walk. Once again, I was carried by the donkey. The weather took a turn for the worse and under howling winds and treacherous snowy conditions, the view of the summit was invisible. The whiteout conditions prohibited us from a promised view of majestic beauty.

The ascent down was easier, as I no longer required the help of the donkey as my breathing began to improve immensely. The sun even surfaced, revealing a beautiful terrain of rugged mountains woven in between emerald lakes and lush shrubs. Every so often I would pass by a group of llamas that were grazing.

I stood in awe before them, realizing they came as a reminder for me to live in that moment no matter how uncomfortable I felt.

On our final day of our hike, we arrived at Machu Picchu early in the morning to catch a glimpse of the sunrise upon this divine place. I was overtaken by the all-encompassing beauty and find it impossible to describe the magnificence that is Machu Picchu because words cannot capture the essence of it. In the words of Krishnamurti and Ade, "the description is not to describe." So I can only emphasize my feelings standing atop this sacred landmark and that is of uninhibited peace.

Even with the place packed full of tourists more concerned with taking selfies than actually being in the moment to enjoy Machu Picchu in all of its glory, I managed to ignore the surrounding madness. I perched myself atop the highest point of Huanya Picchu overlooking Machu Picchu and brought myself into a deep meditative state.

In my meditative state, I was able to reflect that my hike to Machu Picchu wasn't supposed to be easy – I was meant to experience many layers of discomfort in order to parallel it to the experiences of my own life. The hike, with all its twist and turns, inclines and declines, was a metaphor symbolizing the turbulences we all adhere to. The ever-changing weather and landscapes throughout the hike—starting from the plush green forest to the rolling hills to the barren ridges—epitomizes the impermanence of life and enhances the sentiment that things around you will continually change. But the only thing that can remain constant is you.

Looking back, I'm so grateful that I spent most of the hike alone. The truth is, we all walk this journey called life alone, but in our direst times, the universe does send us help. Marcus, the guide, and the donkey were my saviors when I could no longer move. They gave me hope to continue on. Every step I walked, regardless of how tantalizing, signified me leaving my past behind – stepping away from the darkness and into the light of the future.

Machu Picchu sits nestled above the sky, at the highest point where you're closest to the sun. The Incas worship the sun god, Inti, because she represents life. Life revolves around the sun, and without it, life perishes.

I was summoned to stand upon a place where life begins and ends, indicative of my journey coming full circle. In a moment of solitude, a voice inside me spoke ever so loudly: "Your past stays on this mountain, for when you come down, you will become a new person. You will become light."

I opened my eyes and gazed out at the power that is Machu Picchu. And I know that my healing transformation is now complete. There is nothing left in me but the emblematic stillness of serenity in its purist.

Made in the USA
Charleston, SC
05 September 2016